DU BOIS

AND EDUCATION

One of the most prominent African American intellectuals of the twentieth century, W. E. B. Du Bois continues to influence the understanding of race relations in the United States. In this deeply personal introduction to the man and his ideas, esteemed scholar Carl A. Grant reflects on how Du Bois's work has illuminated his own life practices as a Black student, teacher, assistant principal, and professor. Sharing the story of a brilliant man's life contribution to teaching about race and the ideologies and methodologies of racism in education and social and political thought, Grant begins his narrative with a broad overview of Du Bois's life and scholarship, before turning more specifically to Du Bois's theory of an educational system. The book concludes with an examination of Du Bois's curriculum model, predicated upon the work of the NAACP, the Harlem Renaissance, and Du Bois's own writings, as well as a discussion of the lasting legacy of Du Bois's educational and social theory in the present day. Ideal for graduate-level courses in curriculum theory, educational foundations, and education history, *Du Bois and Education* provides an in-depth examination of Du Bois's scholarship, social criticism, and political thought as they relate to his educational theory.

Carl A. Grant is Hoefs-Bascom Professor in the Department of Curriculum and Instruction and former Chair of the Afro American Studies Department at the University of Wisconsin–Madison.

Routledge Key Ideas in Education Series

Series Editors: Bob Lingard and Fazal Rizvi
Founding Editors: Greg Dimitriadis and Bob Lingard

Freud and Education, Deborah P. Britzman
Marx and Education, Jean Anyon
Foucault, Power, and Education, Stephen J. Ball
L.S. Vygotsky and Education, Luis C. Moll
Freire and Education, Antonia Darder
Literacy and Education, James Gee
Du Bois and Education, Carl A. Grant

DU BOIS

AND EDUCATION

CARL A. GRANT

Routledge
Taylor & Francis Group

NEW YORK AND LONDON

First published 2018
by Routledge
711 Third Avenue, New York, NY 10017

and by Routledge
2 Park Square, Milton Park, Abingdon, Oxon, OX14 4RN

Routledge is an imprint of the Taylor & Francis Group, an informa business

© 2018 Taylor & Francis

The right of Carl A. Grant to be identified as author of this work has been asserted
by him in accordance with sections 77 and 78 of the Copyright, Designs and Patents
Act 1988.

Library of Congress Cataloging-in-Publication Data
A catalog record for this book has been requested

ISBN: 978-1-138-18915-7 (hbk)
ISBN: 978-1-138-18916-4 (pbk)
ISBN: 978-1-315-64176-8 (ebk)

Typeset in Minion
by Apex CoVantage, LLC

Dedicated to those who embody the enduring passion and relentless spirit of W. E. B. Du Bois and are effectively putting into practice his scholarship and activism against the color line.

CONTENTS

SERIES EDITOR'S INTRODUCTION

This series introduces key people and topics and discusses their particular implications for the field of education. Written by the most prominent thinkers in the field, these "key ideas" are read through the series authors' past and present work, with particular attention given to the ways these ideas can, do, and might impact theory, research, practice, and policy in education.

More specifically, these texts offer particular conversations with prominent authors, whose work has resonated across education and related fields. Books in this series read as conversations with authorities, whose thinking has helped constitute these ideas and their role in the field of education—yesterday, today, and tomorrow.

Much more than introductions alone, these short, virtuosic volumes look to shape ongoing discussions in the field of education by putting the field's contemporary luminaries in dialogue with its foundational figures and critical topics. From new students to senior scholars, these volumes will spark the imaginations of a range of readers thinking through key ideas and education.

PREFACE

> It would be only fair to the reader to say frankly in advance that the attitude of any person toward this story will be distinctly influenced by his [her] theories of the Negro Race.
>
> (Du Bois, 1934/1935)

William Edward Burghardt Ewing Du Bois's observations have been important to how Americans view historical events such as Reconstruction, Jim Crow, segregation, World War I— including the aftermath—World War II, early years of the Civil Rights Movement, and everyday life in the United States and through-out the world. Du Bois's scholarship has enlightened sociology; US and world history; and philosophy, politics, and education, especially for Blacks. Du Bois's concepts and ideas have been illuminating to Blacks in that they have helped Blacks to see and appreciate the beauty and humanity within themselves and to understand what they must do as a people to sustain their well-being.

Writing *Du Bois and Education* afforded me the opportunity to renew my engagement with Du Bois—"Willie"—one that I had begun subconsciously during my youth and consciously and deliberately at times throughout my college and working years. *Du Bois and Education* is a first-person narrative that seeks to share a story of a brilliant man's life contribution to the teaching about race and the ideologies and methodologies of racism in education and social and political thought.

Du Bois and Education discusses Du Bois's influence on me as a youth in Chicago; during my college years in Nashville, Tennessee; as a teacher and assistant principal in a Chicago public school; and as a graduate student and now a professor at University of Wisconsin-Madison (UW). My writing about Du Bois and his work, which took place at a different moment in history and often in a different geographical context than those in which Du Bois lived and worked, gave me the opportunity to draw on Du Bois's major concepts and apply them to my experiences as a Black student, teacher, assistant principal, and professor.

The concepts of Du Bois's that I mostly include are "I am a problem," "the Negro problem," "color line," "propaganda," "veil/Veil," "two-ness," and "double consciousness." Additionally, I use Du Bois's statements and observations to elucidate experiences and events that I discuss and the observations and comments during and throughout the narrative I make, in part, to show the agelessness and universality of his scholarship.

I wrote *Du Bois and Education* during a time when the nightly news and print and social media were reporting on America as a divided country—more divided than ever, according to 77% of the population (Jones, 2016). Also, news reports on global affairs contend that the primarily Western concept of world order is being rejected by other cultures and destabilizing forces, such as terrorism, ethnic cleansing, violence toward women, and global warming, along with the political and economic systems of the world being at variance with one another. The international economic system is global, and the political systems in the world are based on the nation-state concept. In addition, with mayors' offices and public school systems that primarily serve Black and Brown students selling off their Tenth and Fourteenth Amendment responsibilities caused me, on numerous occasions, to ask aloud, "Willie, how would you respond to this national and global unrest and misery, where the humanity of human kind is being blatantly disregarded and the captains of economics, politics, war, anguish, and social upheaval show little or no emotion over the death or brutality heaped on a human who is different than they are?"

The major purpose of *Du Bois and Education* is to reintroduce to school staffs, community groups, and college and university colleagues the germaneness of Du Bois's scholarship and activism at this social and political moment in American and world history. I use a Du Boisian lens to better understand how groups, classes, ideas, values, and political systems (re)produce their space during historical moments (Lefebvre, 1991; Wilson, 2002). I discuss and apply Du Bois's understanding to my work. My first-person narrative, in other words, is a mere vehicle to transport "gentle readers" to Du Bois's ideas, beliefs, and arguments about education and other social and political issues today. Readers of current literature and listeners of media reports will not find my story as a Black man discussing personal and professional experiences with race, racism, and its manifestations particularly unique. However, it is because of the ordinariness of my story of race and racism that Du Bois and Du Boisian theorizing, framings, and concepts can be presented and showcased for their relevance to the here and now.

References

Jones, J. M. (2016). Record-high 77% of Americans perceive nation as divided. *Gallup*. November 21. Available online: www.gallup.com/poll/197828/record-high-americans-perceive-nation-divided (accessed 22 December 2016).

Lefebvre, H. (1991). *The production of space*. Translated by Donald Nicholson-Smith. Oxford: Blackwell.

Wilson, B. M. (2002). "Critically Understanding Race-Connected Practices: A Reading of W. E. B. DuBois and Richard Wright." *The Professional Geographer*, 54(1), 31–41.

ACKNOWLEDGMENTS

A book-writing project often brings to the undertaking wonderful interactions with many who are long remembered and greatly appreciated. Sincere thanks to Alexandra Allweiss for her excellent suggestions throughout the project. Much thanks to Nadine Goff for valuable feedback during the early stages of the writing. Harvey Long has my gratitude for his assistance with references, suggestions on archival materials, and constructive feedback in general. Emily Braun, Anthony Brown, Paul Grant, Brianne Pitts, and Robert Saddler offered valuable comments and suggestions that were greatly appreciated. Much gratitude is extended to Timuel Black for his discussion with me about the history of Chicago and Carter G. Woodson. Heartfelt brotherly love is given to my brothers Alvin and Shelby for putting up with my numerous phone calls to query them and ask for their help in remembering our growing up in Bronzeville, Chicago. MERIT library, as always, continues to be a valuable helper and resource to me when I am seeking articles and other publications that my talents will not allow me to retrieve. Finally, thanks to the students in my "Black Intellectual Thought in Curriculum and Black Lives Matter" graduate class for their questions each week about the book and suggestions about numerous things I was debating with myself about, such as should I lower or uppercase "black and white." Today's scholars got their way.

1

GROWING UP IN THE SUNSHINE OF W. E. B. DU BOIS

Our lives are about the stories we hear, the stories we tell about ourselves and about others, and the narrative thread that results when they are intertwined. Telling, leading, and participating in the story of the social and political development of African Americans was the primary focus of William Edward Burghardt Du Bois's life. Born in Great Barrington, Massachusetts, in 1868, Du Bois became a teacher, philosopher, sociologist, scholar, and political activist. His first book, *The Philadelphia Negro*, was the first case study of a Black community in the United States. Filled with graphs and statistics, it was an early and innovative example of statistically based social science. His next book, *The Souls of Black Folk*, combines ideologies, methodologies, histories, and critiques of race and racism. *Souls* introduced important ideas and concepts and terms that illuminated the thinking of Du Bois's generation about theorizing about race and racism, and it continues to be relevant to the discussion of race and race relations today, and it will likely remain so in the future. When one considers America's greatest intellectuals, W. E. B. Du Bois must be on the short list.

Writing *Du Bois and Education* was presented to me by my editor and my publisher. The idea was not to regurgitate Du Bois's scholarship and ideas, but to address the effects his work and life had on me personally and professionally. I was humbled by the invitation, but it brought with it challenges that I needed to consider. How had this great fighter for racial equality affected my life? I had never thought about it directly. I had learned about Du Bois as a child and read his publications in college. I found his writing illuminating and informative, and much of what he said about race was in line with my own thinking and action, and that of my immediate and extended family. I drew on his work as a professional, and in some cases expanded on, responded to, and critiqued his ideas. I knew writing *Du Bois and Education* would also be a challenge, because Du Bois and I lived at different times, grew up in different locations, experienced different personal and professional opportunities, held different thoughts about the development of Black leadership, and had different values about recognizing and supporting women as equals in scholarship and humanity. Also, I knew from reading Du Bois that race and racism are best understood in their proper historical context and in their appropriate geographical context. Groups, classes, ideas, values, and political systems produce their space at particular historical moments (Lefebvre, 1991; Wilson, 2002) That said, Du Bois and I were two of a kind in thinking about the value of education and the role education can play in one's life, and how it can and should be used to serve others.

Du Bois was born midway through the nineteenth century, and I was born decades into the twentieth century. Du Bois's formative years (before he went to Fisk University in Nashville, Tennessee) were in the small New England town of Great Barrington. Du Bois was the only Black student in his high school graduating class of 16. He did not meet and exchange ideas with a large group of educated Black male and female students on a regular basis until he attended Fisk at the age of 17. Throughout his education (including Fisk, Harvard, and the University of Berlin), he was taught by White teachers and faculty. He did not experience Blacks in leadership positions during his formative years. His primary, and probably only, role model of Black manhood and progress when he was young was his grandfather, Burghardt. Du Bois (1925) describes his grandfather in the following way: "Always he held his head high, took no insults, made few friends. He was not a 'Negro'; he was a man!" (p. 18). About his father, Du Bois states,

> My father, bent before grandfather, but did not break—better if he had. He yielded and flared back, asked forgiveness and forgot why, became the harshly-held favorite, who ran away and rioted and roamed and loved and married my brown mother.

During his early childhood, Du Bois (1925) states his father "began his restless wanderings . . . [and] soon faded out of our lives into silence" (p. 19).

I was taught by Black and White teachers in elementary school and high school, and by an all-Black faculty as an undergraduate at Tennessee State University (TSU) in Nashville, Tennessee. My years before heading off to college were spent in Bronzeville, a seven-mile-long and one-mile-wide striving Black community in Chicago. Bronzeville is noted for numerous Black leaders, male and female, who set up a bank, hospital, shops, grocery stories, insurance company, women's hair product company, library, art center, newspapers, restaurants, housing, and other establishments to be self-sufficient and enterprising. It was after high school at the University of Illinois at Chicago, while working on my MA at Loyola University in Chicago and my PhD at UW, that I experienced being taught by an all-White faculty. Unlike, Du Bois, I was blessed to have numerous role models of Black men and women: The Grants, as they were collective called, according to formal and informal accounts, were good, friendly, caring people. Most of the family members were educated: professionally trained in medicine, dentistry, engineering, and the arts. Although they had different takes on life as Blacks and on the way to actualize their humanity, the one common goal they all had was education, which anchored their lives and Du Bois's life.

Episodic Memory: I Am Still, "Going Backward to Move Forward"

Significant to writing and reading *Du Bois and Education* is understanding that the stories I tell took place at different points of time in my life, and I am drawing on different pieces (e.g., events and places) of Du Bois's life and writings that may not necessarily match up (time-wise) with my own, but they do speak to and illuminate my experiences and the experiences of others who grew up doing my time. No chronological comparison is intended. In addition, I draw on Du Bois to point out (1) how people were talking about Du Bois during my childhood and how their discussion shaped my thinking then and/or how Du Bois's theorizing permeated a lot of the discourse and ways of thinking at the time in explicit and implicit ways and (2) how Du Bois's theorizing and insights about race, racism, and activism guided my understandings about who I am and what I have experienced regarding race and racism in America. Stories of Du Bois that I heard when I was young in many ways served as the outside validation of race and racism, as well as the potential of American democracy I was hearing about in my home.

Episodic memory is the memory of autobiographical events (times, places, emotions, and other contextual who, what, when, where, and why knowledge that can be explicitly stated) (Tulving, 1972). It is the collection of past personal experiences that occurred at a particular time and place. Tulving (1972) argues that there are three key properties of episodic memory recollection: subjective sense of time (or mental time travel), connection to the self, and autonoetic consciousness. Autonoetic consciousness refers to a special kind of consciousness that accompanies the act of remembering, which enables an individual to be aware of the self in a subjective time (Tulving, 1972).

"Digging up" my own history stirred up old emotions and memories. I recalled tensions or disagreements I had with Du Bois's ideas, such as the "Talented Tenth," and his professional relations with women colleagues. "Digging up" required often phoning relatives and friends in Chicago to discuss the times when we were growing up and the conservations we had about race. I would ask when and where they first heard of Du Bois and in what context. Some friends', and my two older brothers', phones rang much more often than usual and at the oddest times. Relatives and friends helped me flesh out context and recall incidents and events. Shelby, the historian in the family, who has all the family's archives, remembers some events in my life far better than I do. My friend Bob migrated to Chicago with his family from Chattanooga, Tennessee, when he was young, but he remembered the migration. I asked Bob to tell me about his experiences, if any, with racism in the North and South, and when he first heard of Du Bois and in what context. I contacted historians who specialize in the history of Bronzeville and the study of Chicago urban realism. I reread *Black Metropolis, A Study of Negro Life in a Northern City* (Chicago) by St. Clair Drake and Horace Cayton (1945/1962/1970), which addresses in its 857 pages the development of a great Black metropolis and describes the relationship between Blacks and Whites, and the civic, economic, and social development of Blacks living in an isolated, segregated, urban community as well as the impact of this twin configuration upon the social, intellectual, and political well-being, as well as institutional structure, of African Americans in Chicago. In addition, I read and reread many of Du Bois's publications and visited online archives that house his work.

I spoke to friends who lived in Madison about life and conditions in the city and on the University of Wisconsin campus for people of color during the time I arrived to begin graduate school in 1969. Madisonians, whom I have gotten to know over the years, were helpful with information about the history of Madison and life, policies, and practices on the UW campus. Retrieving documents at the Wisconsin State Historical Society archives helped me too and enabled me to "return" to the time of my arrival on the Madison campus in 1969 via newspaper articles and film footage. Also, the information librarians at MERIT helped me to locate publications when I didn't have the complete citations.

Four places of episodic memory are my home at 3133 Prairie Avenue, the South Side Community Art Center, George Cleveland Hall Library, and the YMCA at 3763 South Wabash.

In these places, I engaged with Du Bois consciously and without my knowing how he was influencing me as a person and what I have now become.

Beginning the Story

I was a child of parents who were a part of the Great Migration (1915–1970) to Chicago from the South. My mother, Nellie, came to Chicago from Huntsville, Alabama, during the 1920s to join her two older sisters, Alice and Gussie. Alice did "day work" for a White family on the north side of the city, and Gussie (we called her Tish) worked as a maid in the Stevens Hotel (now the Hilton Hotel) on Michigan Avenue. Upon arriving in Chicago, Nellie enrolled in Wendell Phillips High School to complete her high school education. Phillips is also the high school that three of her four sons would attend. Wendell Phillips (1811–1884), an abolitionist and fighter for the rights of American Indians, was the person featured in Du Bois's high school graduation address. About his valediction address, Du Bois (1920) posits, "This was my first sweet taste of the world's applaud time" (p. 7).

My father, Alvin Grant, was a migrant to Chicago from Bainbridge, Georgia. He was drafted into WWI shortly after he arrived. In the army, Alvin served in France as part of a machine gun squad in a Black battalion. He was in the Battle of Argonne Forest in France, which lasted from September 26 to November 11, 1918, when the Armistice to end the war was signed. Dad told me he was on the front line of battle in Argonne Forest, which historians describe as the bloodiest operation of WWI, and believed he would have been killed on November 11 if the Armistice had not been signed. When I asked him why he thought that way, he said, "I was a machine gunner, and my squad was under orders to advance on November 11, and the German troops always wanted to take out the machine gunners as soon as possible." The Battle of Argonne, I believe, through the stories Dad told, influenced his view of life. It made him less uptight than his older brothers, but at the same time, the experience made him hold firm to the goal to pursue his education and to do good for others in remembrance of his soldier buddies who were killed or severely wounded. My father attended Morris Brown College in Atlanta, followed by Meharry Dental School in Nashville, Tennessee, after his honorable discharge. His older brothers, James and William, attended Wilberforce College followed by Meharry Medical School. Both James and William modeled Du Bois in dress, including the wearing of spats, but they did not carry canes. My father, unlike his brothers, didn't dress in a Du Boisian style, which was the style of the day. His clothes were less formal and his manner was easygoing. When I asked my father why he too didn't choose medicine like his two brothers, he told me, "At first I had planned to become a doctor like your uncles James and William, but during the war, I saw too much blood and death, so I decided to go dental school instead." In 1923, after his graduation from Meharry, my father moved back to Chicago.

My father's sister, Cloe Ezelle, graduated from Fisk University, which was the same college Du Bois attended and across the street from Meharry Medical and Dental College. She was proud of her matriculation at Fisk, in part because it was considered the academically top-ranked university for Blacks to attend. She also sung with the Fisk Jubilee singers and traveled nationally and internationally with its world-famous choir. Cloe Ezelle taught piano professionally, and she taught my two older brothers how to play. I had no interest in learning to play the piano, and at times today, I still regret not taking advantage of the opportunity.

Between James, William, Alvin, and Cloe Ezelle, the latter was the one I describe as outwardly promoting the idea of the "Talented Tenth." However, Cloe Ezelle would have taken Du Bois to the woodshed for not including women in the "Talented Tenth." I know she and many of her Fisk friends that I met over the years had to wonder about Du Bois's reasoning because, according to her and her friends, many, many smart women attended and graduated from Fisk. The students Cloe Ezelle taught piano were predominately girls of varying ages. Many times, I heard her encouraging them to go to college. "Don't think about marriage after high school," she would say. "Go to college."

My father's parents, Leah and Alvin, arrived in Chicago in 1917. Alvin senior worked on the railroad, while Leah worked to take care of the house and her children and grandchildren. She was a quiet force, who encouraged her children to get an education. The Grants believed, like Du Bois (1944), that "the secret of life and the loosing of the color bar . . . lay in excellence, in accomplishment" (p. 33). However, they did not believe, as Du Bois said his mother did, that "there was no discrimination because of color—it was all a matter of ability and hard work" (Du Bois, 1944, p. 33).

My father met my mother in Chicago after he returned from dental school. They were married in 1924. A year later, my brother Alvin was born; three years later, Shelby was born; and five years later, I came screaming into the world. Ernest was born four years after that. My brothers and I grew up in a very happy family. We ate dinner together every night. On Sunday, we often had oysters for breakfast—a favorite of my father's. Ernest couldn't stand the smell of oysters, so he would retreat to the front porch. Then it was off to Sunday School for the sons and church for my mother and father. However, my father attended a Methodist church, for that was the church he'd attended growing up. My mother attended Pilgrim Baptist church, for that was the church she'd attended growing up. After church, besides preparing a Sunday dinner, we made homemade ice cream: a different flavor each week.

Bob, a good friend I will introduce in the next chapter, once said to me when we were in college discussing Du Bois and the "Talented Tenth," "Carl, that's your family." I recall just looking at Bob, not knowing what to say, being shy, and not wanting to reply directly. I understood what Bob was saying about my family, but Du Bois's elitism, some of his harsh but honest language from his perspective about Blacks, I didn't want to identify with. It was not in line with what my brothers and I had learned from my mother about speaking about people, both Black and White. That said, Du Bois's belief in an academic education, racial uplift, racial equality, a strong belief in the humanity of Blacks, Pan-Africanism, and service to others was my daily bread. I never consciously acknowledged or spoke directly to my friends about it, but I ate it daily at 3133 Prairie, and it went down easy.

The house where we lived up through my high school years was in Chicago's Bronzeville. Between 1915 and 1940, thousands of Blacks migrated to Chicago and into Bronzeville to escape violence and segregation in the South. Bronzeville was earlier referred to as the "Black Belt" and the "Black Metropolis." Bronzeville was a striving community; the children of the early Black migrants, along with other new arrivals, became artists, musicians, businessmen, politicians, entrepreneurs, and, in later years, millionaires. My immediate neighborhood and the block that I lived on were inhabited by a mixture of educationally and economically diverse Black people. People got along well with one another. My mother told my brothers and me from a very early age to be nice and polite to all, and as we saw her do it, we followed along. Neighbors reached out to one another for help. Hierarchical status and privilege were rarely showcased; one's profession only came into play as a service and help. My uncles and father often performed medical and dental services without expecting a penny. Each year, there was a block party in the summertime and decorating of the block with a common theme for Christmas. Every adult on my block was my parent, and none hesitated to exercise their authority. I couldn't get away with anything.

When I read Du Bois's accounts of growing up in Great Barrington, I recall initially thinking I had the better of the two experiences growing up because I lived in a "bubble." The Black neighborhood where I lived shielded me from the mercurial behavior of Whites that Du Bois had to contend with growing up in Great Barrington. My motivation for academic excellence was not to "best" students in my class because of their skin color, privilege, or way they treated me. Also, I did not experience a girl refusing my gift because she falsely thought my race was inferior and that she was superior to me. However, years later, I questioned my "bubble" thinking. I knew I lived in a racist world, behind a veil. But later I came to understand I was in a "Veil/prison" with walls so tall they were unassailable, despite having graduated from a world-class university and developing the ability to communicate as well as Whites can, if not better, about societal problems and issues, especially those in urban communities. My humanity, I learned, was not accepted as equal to White humanity. The White gaze would continually look upon me and other Blacks with a glee of superiority. Therefore, because of my Black body, and *not* my academic preparation, social economic status, education, success of my family, and service to others, I was assigned to live my academic and personal life in the Veil: I too am a "problem."

It is important to point out that Du Bois, as Sawyer (n. d.) writes, discussed Veil, capital "V" and lowercase "v." Veil and veil are two concepts used to refer to Blacks who live behind the color line. Second sight, double consciousness, and two-ness are related to the veil. Reading Du Bois, I understood the concepts of "double consciousness" and "veil" are two deeply connected concepts that Du Bois introduced to help Blacks understand and express the pain and frustration that comes with living in a racist society. Du Bois, explaining the veil, noted the black or darker skin of Black people marks them as physically different than Whites; the veil prevents Whites from seeing Blacks as "true" Americans, and the veil addresses Blacks' inability to see themselves outside of what Whites describe and prescribe for them.

Du Bois (1903a) used the concept "two-ness" in speaking about how Black people thought about themselves in connection to their country: born as "outcasts and strangers"—in America—in my "mine own house" (p. 2). Du Bois (1903a), describing this ambivalent feelings about Blacks, states, "One ever feels his two-ness,— an American, a Negro, two souls, two thoughts, two unreconciled striving; two warring ideals in one dark body, whose dogged strength alone keeps it from being torn asunder" (p. 2). During the early decades after Emancipation, throughout World War I and II and the Civil Rights Movement, and some may argue today, "two-ness" was a feeling, an attitude of uncertainty, Blacks were forced to endure. My dad spoke of it when he said to me,

> We—Black soldiers during WWI—at times, wondered aloud, as we readied for a battle that would certainly bring death to some of us,

if not all of us—why? As Americans . . . we were constantly reminded by Whites that we were not equal to them, and although we wore the US uniform, America was not really our home, like it was the home of White people.

In 2014, when I heard about "I, Too, Am Harvard" and saw the photos and read the interviews of minority students' alienation, loneliness, and negative experiences in social interactions with other students on the campus, I recalled the meaning of my father's words: Black people don't escape the racism, the US uniform notwithstanding: "a stranger in my own house."

According to Du Bois, "double consciousness" informs the "two-ness" of being "an American and an African American," thus enabling Blacks to have the ability to move almost unconsciously between the two identities. Furthermore, because of their historical experience of living in a White racist society, Blacks can navigate the White world and the Black world better than Whites. Du Bois describes this ability as a "gift" Black people, but not White, have that allows them to see the great potential of America. The veil, however, references Blacks' inability to see themselves outside of the way Whites see them and position them.

At Fisk, soaking up academic and social knowledge and living around smart, young Black men and women for the first time in his life, Du Bois (1903) writes of being with the learned Black people who reside in the Veil: "I who speak here am bone of the bone and flesh of the flesh of them that live within the Veil" (p. 6). Sawyer (n.d.) states,

It is clear that, beyond the Veil cannot be confused with the spaces outside of the color line. Were that to be the case, Du Bois would have been seeking [when he taught in Tennessee] to teach a diverse group of students, not just blacks deprived of educational opportunities.

(p. 11; for an excellent discussion of "V" and "v"eil, please see, Michael Sawyer (n. d.) The Duboisian V[v]eil{s} Reex)

After I graduated high school, I attended the University of Illinois at Chicago (UIC) for a few weeks. I was one of only a few Blacks among a sea of Whites and Whiteness. I was no longer in my Bronzeville bubble. I immediately experienced racial microaggressions; the color line in this university setting was everywhere. I ate alone in the cafeteria at UIC, and in class, there were usually several empty seats around me. I was invisible to White professors. I left UIC and headed to TSU, an HBCU in Nashville, Tennessee, in part because Alvin and Shelby, my older brothers, asked me why I was tolerating "that racist crap" at UIC. They argued, along with my mother, that I should leave UIC. A year or so later at TSU reading *Souls*, I saw my experience at UIC through Du Bois's experiences. In "Of the Meaning a Progress," an essay that I will return to in Chapter 4, Du Bois characterized my attitude when I entered UIC and came face-to-face with White classmates and faculty; many didn't think I belonged there, and they didn't want me there. Du Bois writes about teaching Black sharecroppers' children in the rural areas of Tennessee during the summer months when he was a third-year student at Fisk. "I was a Fisk student, then and all Fisk men thought that Tennessee, beyond the Veil was theirs alone, and during vacation time they sallied forth in lusty bands to meet the country commissions" of schools to teach Black children and youth (p. 46). Du Bois infers that, with his university learning, he had torn away the veil, crossed the color line, and earned the right to be treated equally.

When I entered UIC after a nice write-up in the *Chicago Tribune* as a top student in my high school, like Du Bois, I too probably "sallied forth." I came to UIC knowing I could do the work and wanting to enjoy the fruits of college life that I had heard about for many years at my dinner table and in discussions with uncles and aunts. However, like Du Bois, my bubble busted, and I learned that despite being an excellent academic student with the achievable aspirational of becoming a doctor, I was, nevertheless, confined to the Veil. Black-and-Brown educated people are prevented from entering the so-called White world. Sawyer (n. d.) states,

> The separation between white and black remains unaffected in its integrity by the project of education. Black Subject remains imprisoned inside of the Veil of Race/Color because this improved educated, knowledgeable subject/black person is prevented from fulfilling her or his promise.
>
> (pp. 10–11)

A message often given in the Black community to youth is that, regardless of how smart or qualified for a position you are, your Blackness may prevent you from receiving it. In addition, your racial identity may cause you to not be included. Du Bois experienced exclusion several times during his youth, and each time, although it struck him hard, it gave him determination.

Du Bois explains,

> "Come in," said commissioner—"come in. Have a seat. Yes, that certificate will do. Stay to dinner. What do you want a month?" "Oh." Thought I, "this is lucky," but even then fell the awful shadow of the Veil, for they ate first, and then I-alone.
>
> (1903a, p. 48)

My early dream of becoming a doctor was supported by my father and his brothers. They believed their family members could achieve their professional goals and often told us so. Aunt Cloe Ezelle, my father's sister who had graduated from Fisk University, strongly encouraged us. She would say, "If you study hard and get good grades, you can attend Fisk or Wilberforce, where your uncles attended, or Morris Brown, where your father attended." My mother and her sisters kept my brothers and me socially and political grounded. They explained structural racism and microaggressions before there were such words. The sisters helped us understand that Blacks were considered "the problem" because of White people's insatiable desire for power, opportunity, and wealth. Du Bois (1920) put into his words what my mother and her sisters were saying: "Wave on wave, each with increasing virulence, is dashing this new religion of Whiteness on the shores of our time" (p, 18). My mother told stories of the horrors of structural racism in a way that I could "feel and see" the inhumanity in segregation and the effects of Jim Crow. Always speaking softly and drawing on events that had taken place throughout history, she would also talk to us about current events taking place in Chicago, which she considered teachable moments. I recall as a little kid learning about how accomplishments by a Black person served as a source of racial pride and how failures by a Black worked in the opposite way.

In 1938, on a hot night in June, Black boxer Joe Louis knocked-out White boxer Max Schmeling in the first round of their second fight. Louis's victory caused my neighbors to erupt with joy. Blacks streamed out of their homes. They paraded up-and-down the street. Happily, they loudly banged pots and pans, blew car horns, whistled, and shouted. I asked my mother, "Why are the grown-ups acting like children?" She laughed and explained that Joe Louis's superiority over a White man in the boxing ring was a source of great pride to Black people. "He was not only fighting for himself, but all Black people, including you."

Years later, I came across a poem by Langston Hughes that gave my mother's words a broader context for my understanding. I learned that World Heavyweight Champion Joe Louis lost his first fight to Schmeling two years earlier, and Blacks had felt disheartened, some even fearful. Louis was a living symbol to Blacks, of Black humanity, and Blacks equality to Whites, something they knew, but had few opportunities to point out. Also, Louis's boxing skills point out that Whites are not infallible. Whites are not superior. Louis was Black people's most visible symbol of hope and dreams that pushed back on the Negro as a problem thesis. However, when he lost his first fight to Max Schmeling, the Black community across the United States was devastated. Langston Hughes wrote about the misery Blacks were experiencing immediately after the first fight in June 1936: "I walked down Seventh Avenue and saw grown men weeping like children, and women sitting in the curbs with their head in their hands" (Hughes, Rampersad and MacLaren, 2001).

Two years later in 1938, Hughes described what a victory by Joe Louis did for Black striving and how it helped Blacks to be proud of their humanity.

> Each time Joe Louis won a fight in those depression years, even before he became champion, thousands of black Americans on relief or W.P.A., and poor, would throng out into the streets across the land to march and cheer and yell and cry because of Joe's one-man triumphs. No one else in the United States has ever had such an effect on Negro emotions—or on mine. I marched and cheered and yelled and cried, too.
>
> (Hughes, Rampersad and MacLaren, 2001)

Du Bois in My Early Life Story

What follows are some of my stories about growing up in a segregated neighborhood intertwined with stories I heard from others. They are illuminated by examples of how Du Bois and his stance on race, politics, and education influenced our decisions and the narrative arcs of our lives, and made White people pause to understand that Black people's agency and actions to make equal their humanity would never stop. In writing *Du Bois and Education*, I tried to keep in mind the charge from my editor not to regurgitate Du Bois, but to address how Du Bois's ideologies and methodologies of race and racism influenced my personal and professional career as a schoolteacher and administrator in an urban school in Chicago and as a professor of education and Afro American studies. Du Boisian ideology and theorizing were for certain an influence, along with the Grant family.

Stories of Discoveries: My First Sightings of Du Bois

Listening and Learning

I work at listening well; I learned it from being my mother's son. Note-taking is not my strength, in large part because 30 minutes after I write something down, I can't read it. My mother told me when I was in middle school that my handwriting looked like "chicken scratch." She was not exaggerating, nor was she the only person to tell me this. During my freshman year, Ms. Boren, my homeroom teacher, insisted that I take typing. Her words were, "Carl, I know you are going to college. You will need to type your papers for your professors, because they will not be able to read your handwriting." Ms. Boren and her teaching buddy, Ms. Sweeney, kept me in typing classes for four very *long* years, insisting that I keep returning the following semester. My "chicken scratch" handwriting also forced me to learn how to listen well and to recall what I hear. This works on most occasions, except for peoples' names. In working at listening, I have come to enjoy, learn from, and use stories as a major learning and teaching tool.

As a child, I always wanted to know what was going on. Some may have described me as a nosey kid. I would describe myself as curious and precocious. As a child, I listened carefully when adults talked about other adults. W. E. B. Du Bois was a "New Negro," who many adults were talking about and saw as a role model for their children. Du Bois's ideas and statements describing aspects of race and racism—"double consciousness," "the veil," "the color line," and "two-ness" gave Black people ways of thinking about and seeing themselves that spoke to the racial conditions in which they were living. Du Bois's ideas explained feelings and insights Blacks had but didn't have the words to express. Understanding these ideas helped Blacks to understand themselves and each other better, and to understand the struggle they were engaged in; this understanding increased positive thoughts about self and the Black community. Of course, the words or phrases Du Bois used were not always the same ones used by everyday people, but I learned to understand their meanings and effects on Black people collectively and individually. For me, as a young boy, "double consciousness" was the feeling that came with your country not accepting you because of your Black skin, so you saw yourself and measured yourself through White folks' eyes. This I struggled to resist when I attended UIC and was surrounded by a White wall of students. I deliberately saw myself as a successful person who earned his way onto the UIC campus and who grew up in enterprising Bronzeville.

In addition, and more importantly, I knew I was the son of a prideful and strong Black family, whose father could have been killed fighting for the land of their grandparents. I didn't hate them, but I questioned their arrogance and air of superiority. Du Bois (1903a), in the essay, "Souls of White Folk" writes about race, World War I—the War my father fought in—and England, the United States, Italy and Frances's continuation of maintaining colonialization of African countries. His words make me think of my father in battle:

> As we saw the dead dimly through rifts of battle smoke and heard faintly the cursings and accusations of blood brothers, we darker men said: This is not Europe gone mad; this is not aberration nor insanity; this *is* Europe; this seeming Terrible is the real soul of white culture . . . these dark and awful depths and not the shining and ineffable heights of which it boasted.
>
> (p. 22)

"Color line" meant structural racism. I thought of the "color line" as when my mother and her sister had to use a dirty "colored-only toilet" or when my family was not able to eat where we wished when traveling south. Du Bois (1903) defines the color line as follow: "The relation of the darker to the lighter races of men in Asia and Africa, in America and the islands of the sea" (p. 9). These words and expressions were linked by an understanding of the "veil" of racism that separates Blacks having poor jobs and schools, and dying earlier than Whites. Later in college, when I read Du Bois's books and articles, I learned more in-depth definitions of these terms with examples that illustrated their effects. I learned that the concepts of "double consciousness" and "veil" are two deeply connected concepts that Du Bois introduced to help Blacks understand

and express the pain and frustration that come with living in a racist society. Du Bois, explaining the veil, notes the black or darker skin of Black people marks them as physically different than Whites; the veil prevents Whites from seeing Blacks as "true" Americans, and it addresses Blacks' inability to see themselves outside of what Whites describe and prescribe for them.

In the first chapter of *The Souls of Black Folk*, Du Bois describes his first encounter with "the veil" of racism that had heretofore been invisible to him. He was a young Negro boy attending an all-White school where he was "accepted" by the students and their parents. However, one day, it was decided that the students would exchange "visiting-cards." Du Bois describes, "The exchange was merry, till one girl, a tall newcomer, refused my card,—refused it peremptorily, with a glance" (p. 2).

> Then it dawned upon me with a certain suddenness that I was different from the others; or like [them perhaps] in heart and life and longing, but shut out from their world by a vast veil. I had thereafter no desire to tear down that veil, to creep through; I held all beyond it in common contempt, and lived above it in a region of blue sky and great wandering shadows.
>
> (Du Bois, 1903a, p. 2)

Du Bois's use of the concept "two-ness" argues that Blacks better understand Whites than Whites understand Blacks. In other words, Blacks, because of their historical experience of living in a White racist society can navigate the White world and the Black world better than Whites can. Thus, according to Du Bois, "double consciousness" informs the "two-ness" of being "an American and a[n African

American]" and the mostly unconscious, almost natural movement between the two identities. Du Bois writes, "One ever feels his twoness,—an American, a Negro; two souls, two thoughts, two unreconciled strivings; two warring ideals in one dark body, whose dogged strength alone keeps it from being torn asunder" (p. 2). With those words, Du Bois was explaining to Blacks why they might have some negative thoughts about themselves and other Black people because they are Black, or believe a White doctor or lawyer is better than a Black doctor or lawyer. Du Bois explained that during and since enslavement, Blacks have been formally and informally told and taught by Whites through daily contact and interactions and media, as well as the controlling position Whites occupy in society, and so forth, that Whites are better. Blacks should strive to be like them, to judge success and culture based on a White norm.

Du Bois (1903) explained that at the time as he was living behind the color line/veil, he was given the opportunity, as the only Black in his class, to attend school with Whites, but not the liberty to be one of them—that is, to engage with them as a social equal (p. 2).

The reason Du Bois developed these concepts of explanations for Blacks, I understood, grew out of his efforts to point out the desires of Whites to maintain power and have privilege. Du Bois had no thoughts that Blacks were inferior. I too knew from a very early age that my family members were equally as smart as Whites and probably had more, or at least as much, college education as most White families. Inferior, no! Nor were the people whom I met and interacted with throughout Bronzeville. They were smart, and it was their intellectual abilities in all genres imaginable and their striving that caused me to never doubt myself.

The people of Bronzeville who had come to Chicago to escape southern racism, to live in decent housing, to earn a respectful wage, to receive a quality education, to contribute to the war effort, and to live without fear of nighttime Klan raids and being called the "N" word throughout the day singled out Du Bois as a Black who spoke with scientific reason, passion, and urgency of the need for Blacks to redress racial and class inequities. Citizens of Bronzeville had first-hand knowledge of southern terrorism, of having no or little schooling for themselves and their children, of dirty water fountains, and of having to put up with disrespect and humiliation as they rode segregated trains and buses. They spoke in outrage about seeing Black bodies hanging on trees—the "Strange Fruit" Black singer Billy Holiday (1915–1959) vocalized in the 1930s. They had read or heard about Ida B. Wells (1862–1931), a former enslaved woman and one of the founders of the National Association for the Advancement of Colored People (NAACP). They knew of Wells's pamphlets *Southern Horrors: Lynch Law in All Its Phrases* (1892) and *The Red Record* (1895) that described lynching in the United States since Emancipation. Some paraphrased Wells's (1892) words after her good friend Thomas Moss was lynched and said that her message was an impetus for leaving the South. Wells (1892) wrote,

> There is, therefore, only one thing left to do; save our money and leave a town which will neither protect our lives and property, nor give us a fair trial in the courts, but takes us out and murders us in cold blood when accused by white persons.

Wells and Du Bois at times collaborated on scholarly activities. Both were concerned and spoke passionately against lynching.

However, Wells became vexed with Du Bois for leaving her name off the list of original founders of the NAACP.

Bronzevillians spoke of times of fear when the Klan and other forms of White oppression and violence would spontaneously erupt. I learned that Whites would lynch Blacks for the slightest of reasons, such as failing to pay a bill on time, not moving over as they walked by, competing with Whites economically, and being drunk in public (Wells, 1892). I listened silently to stories and information shared often through tears, anger, and sadness. One day, a story that included the gruesome details about lynchings described by a resident of Waco, Texas, in a letter printed in the May 1916 edition of the *Chicago Defender* produced a shaper reaction from my mother than usual.

> Accused of the murder of a white woman several miles from his home, Washington was convicted by a jury despite scant evidence. Then, as happened all too often, Washington was dragged from the courtroom, hung from a tree, and burned on a funeral pyre. "The crowd was made up of some of the supposed best citizens of the South," the letter writer noted. "Doctors, lawyers, business men and Christians (posing as such, however). After the fire subsided, the mob was not satisfied: They hacked with pen knives the fingers, the toes, and pieces of flesh from the body, carrying them as souvenirs to their automobiles."

After the story concluded, I heard my mother say, "I am not taking my children south to visit their relatives until they fully understand the history of where they are going. I don't intend to have any of my sons lynched." While stories of White terrorism were frightening to my friends and me, they taught us that because we were Black, we needed to be extra careful, even living in the North; we should not go wandering into any White neighborhoods; we should not swim in areas of Lake Michigan where Whites swam, and we should be aware that policemen were often not Black people's friends (the "To Protect and Serve," motto used by the Chicago Police Department was for White people).

During those times when Du Bois was discussed, he was portrayed as very intelligent and an activist. People understood that Du Bois's philosophy of political militancy to secure equality with Whites had clashed with Booker T. Washington's philosophy of not agitating for voting and civil rights. Washington argued that Blacks should accept the accommodationist "go-low" policy of White people. Blacks who had witnessed or experienced racial brutality and lynchings saw Du Bois as a "New Negro"—an educated and sophisticated Black who demanded human and civil rights, and challenged discrimination, stereotyping, and any form of racism.

The stories encouraged my friends and me to monitor our behavior around White people and to understand that although we could be in the right, we were considered wrong because we were Black. As Du Bois sarcastically stated, "Whiteness is the ownership of the earth forever and ever. Amen!" (1920, p. 18). My friends and I frequently revisited the stories of race and racism, and Blacks' resiliency and action toward it when we were together. In doing so, at a very young age, we came to realize that "the color line" and the ideas that Blacks were a problem and that "black was bad" were screwed up! White people were the problem!

In college, when I read the words "to the real question, How does it feel to be a problem? I answer seldom a word" (Du Bois, 1903, p. 2), it brought another feeling of validation to my long-held idea that Whites, not Blacks, were the problem. And Du Bois's response, "I answer seldom a word," illustrated that Du Bois knew that "racial segregation is not just a historical or structural condition of twentieth century America—it is a subjective experience" (Social Theory, rewired, n. d.) that places one behind a veil or causes one to live in the Veil.

The debate between Du Bois and Booker T. Washington over the goals of education for Blacks was decades old by the time I entered school. However, because many Blacks were not employed, or they were underemployed, and many had less than a high school education, the two different points of view were often discussed. Washington's argument that education for Black young adults should be "crafts, industrial and farming skills and the cultivation of the virtues, patience, enterprise, and thrift," sounded good to some Blacks who were struggling and coming to see the necessity of education. Du Bois's counterargument that social change for Blacks should be accomplished by pushing forward, not going slow; demanding democratic rights; and being led by college-educated Blacks, the "Talented Tenth," appealed to most others. Whereas both Du Bois and Washington's ideas were positive about Blacks lifting themselves up, Du Bois's argument that Blacks are equal to Whites more strongly challenged White racism. Du Bois (*The Crisis*, 1920) stated,

> We believe that social equality, by a reasonable interpretation of the words, mean moral, mental and physical fitness to associate with one's fellowmen. In this sense THE CRISIS believes absolutely in the Social Equality of the Black and White and Yellow races and it believes too that any attempt to deny this equality by law or custom is a blow at Humanity, Religion and Democracy.

(p. 16)

"Other Suns"

Richard Wright famously described Blacks who were leaving the South and traveling to the North as part of the Great Migration, traveling to the "warmth of other suns." I learned many things about race, racism, and Du Bois seated at the feet of migrants who had traveled to the "warmth of the Bronzeville sun." They told stories of their migration to Chicago. They told of letters from relatives and friends inviting them to leave the racist South and come to the North. Some spoke of how notices in the *Chicago Defender* encouraged them to come to the North. While the stories I heard were different, they had many similarities: anxiety about leaving the South, the unknowns in northern cities, and concerns about finding jobs. Their stories told of their fear of leaving their families, friends, and churches behind. Leaving their churches behind was especially hard for older migrants. Would they be able to "drink of new and cool rains [and] bend in strange winds?" (Wright, 1941, p. 12). Older Blacks knew that for many of them, their first meaningful acknowledgment of freedom was worshiping without fear or without the "master" being nearby. Black migrants also spoke passionately about their children and grandchildren receiving an education. For them, they dreamed of schooling that lasted for months, rather than just a few weeks, and a schoolhouse designed for children's learning, not a place that previously held animals or some agricultural crop. Black parents wanted their children to have books (more than one), a blackboard, and other supplies. Du Bois's idea of the "Talented Tenth," that one in ten Black men should become a leader to "save" Black people, was an idea that many of my neighbors and the Grant family did not endorse. Instead, they believed that all Black children could successfully achieve and all had leadership potential or a talent. The question, or "problem," for many of the people in my neighborhood was acquiring enough money to send their children to college or to a vocational school. My relatives, especially Aunt Cloe Ezelle, were the neighborhood go-to people to talk to about attending college. She was an ambassador for HBCUs. Aunt Cloe Ezelle was the one who encouraged Alvin to attend TSU, and my other brothers and I followed.

Years later, when I came across a statement by Du Bois's stepson about the "Talented Tenth" that stated, before his death, Du Bois reconsidered the numeracy and the elitism of the "Talented Tenth," concept. David Du Bois wrote, "Dr. Du Bois' conviction is that it's those who suffered most and have the least to lose that we should look to for our steadfast, dependable and uncompromising leadership" (quoted in Joy James, 1997). Similarly, L'Monique King (2013) posited:

> Toward the end of William Edward Burghardt Du Bois's life, he too acknowledged the need for redefining his Talented Tenth theory to be one which was more inclusive. His theory took on a "double consciousness" of its own in that he came to believe and understand that "the souls of Black folks" stood to be in consistent conflict if the Black community could not be elevated with the intellectual elite working together with the masses. Unfortunately, this metamorphosis in ideology is one he is infrequently credited with—particularly through the lens of those who are comfortable seeing him as no more than an academic elitist. Though, the term may not be as relevant today as it was when it was conceived, the mission is just as valuable.
>
> (p. 7)

Additionally, the "Talented Tenth" was not Du Bois's own idea. Per Henry Louis Gates Jr., referencing Evelyn Brooks

Higginbotham, "Du Bois borrowed the concept of the "Talented Tenth" from Henry Lyman Morehouse (the man for whom the great Morehouse College was named) seven years before Du Bois popularized it" (p. 1). Morehouse defined the term as follows:

> In the discussion concerning Negro education we should not forget the talented tenth man. An ordinary education may answer for the nine men of mediocrity; but if this is all we offer the talented tenth man, we make a prodigious mistake.
>
> (p. 1)

Morehouse adds, "The tenth man, with superior natural endowments, symmetrically trained and highly developed, may become a mightier influence, a greater inspiration to others than all the other nine, or nine times nine like them" (p. 1). That said, and although I am critical of Du Bois's employment of the "Talented Tenth" and argue that he should have initially promoted higher education for all Blacks, I also believe that Du Bois's primary goal was to get more Blacks educated at the university/college level at a time when few were receiving higher education. In addition, I believe Du Bois's fight with Washington's industrial education thesis encouraged Du Bois to accept the smaller victory of a "Talented Tenth." Finally, my critique of Du Bois is perhaps as much about him staying with the "Talented Tenth" thesis for decades and not eliminating it as soon as he saw the numbers of Blacks receiving a higher education on the rise.

In college, I learned that the migration stories I heard as a child had other meanings. Besides being stories about Blacks' journey north, they were about the rise of Black communities in Midwestern and Northeastern cities—communities where

Black intellectual thought and ideas developed in politics, social relations, education, arts, commerce, and in all others areas. This could be seen in the construction of hospitals, the opening of banks, the building of churches, the establishment of businesses, the development of art centers, and the rise of youth centers in Black communities. In 1917, Du Bois observed that the effect of a quarter million African Americans' migration to the North after 1910 was a social evolution. Du Bois (1917) stated, "The mass of the freedmen is changing rapidly the economic basis of their social development" (p. 4). Living in Bronzeville decades later as a pre-teen, I observed the social development Du Bois wrote about. As migration continued, the rapid growth and development of Bronzeville was like nothing people living in my neighborhood had seen before. The community became increasingly self-sufficient. In my home, there was less of a need for my mother to send one of her sons downtown to shop for grocery items or to purchase clothes. A variety of businesses opened in our community, including insurance agencies, restaurants, well-stocked grocery stories, clothing stores for men and women, stores that catered to babies and young children, barbershops, beauty salons, and places of entertainment and nightlife. Organizations also developed, such as the YMCA, churches, and the Urban League, and my friends and I had three movie theaters in walking distance.

Because of migration, I met two lifelong friends, Lornie and Bob, and many new classmates. Lornie's and Bob's families came north to Chicago from Drew, Mississippi, and Chattanooga, Tennessee, respectively, to enjoy the "warmth of other suns." I listened and learned from their stories of living in the South and moving to the North. In college, reading Du Bois's essays published in *The Crisis* during the days of Great

Migration helped me to better understand the political and sociological dynamics that were associated with the movement north. I would ask Lornie, Bob, and other college classmates I met at TSU who grew up in the South, questions that reading articles in *The Crisis* and reading Du Bois's essays raised in my mind. I was interested in migration stories and stories from my classmates about what their parents and grandparents told them about sharecropping, Black churches in rural areas, and the Klan. I wanted to know how they felt drinking from a Black-only water fountain, or climbing up to the upper balcony of a movie theater to watch a film. Also, I was interested in their stories about living in areas where overt segregation and Jim Crow controlled life and a lie by a White woman could get one lynched. I recall once when I was resisting going to the movies off campus because we would have to sit in the balcony, and because I was fearful, a friend who had lived all of her life in the South told me, "Carl, that's the way of life in the South. Let's go. You will see and feel, what I have lived all of my life."

Like Du Bois, although I had traveled south with my mother when I was young, Nashville was the place where I consciously experienced southern racism as a pre-adult. I would always read Du Bois's essays where he referenced Tennessee, Nashville, and Fisk with special interest. In Nashville, I became a fan of reading newspapers, mostly every day, and in doing so, I read stories and news that had a southern racist perspective that I hadn't overtly seen in Chicago's newspapers. I wondered, during my class on Du Bois, how reading stories published in Nashville newspapers and living in Tennessee influenced the development of Du Bois's ideology and methodologies on race and racism.

Social Darwinism, Pan-Africanism, and Tarzan

Listening to grown-ups in my neighborhood, I learned early that Whites thought they were more intelligent than Blacks. I heard that White people believed that they could do *anything* and *everything* better than Blacks and other people of color; however, I heard numerous stories that said this was not so! Some of those stories were funny, such as the "Trickster stories" that told of enslaved people outsmarting their White oppressors. Many stories were sad because Blacks didn't always win, and the stories pointed out how Whites used their power to keep the color line in place. Such is the case in Du Bois's (1903) "Of the Coming of John." In the story, John, a northern-educated Black man returns to his home in the South and opens a school for Blacks. However, he is reprimanded because he uses a progressive curriculum. Judge Henderson, the White authority of the town, tells John that he has overstepped his bounds, because he is teaching racial equality. The judge exercised White authority by severely scolding John, telling him,

> John . . . in this country the Negro must remain subordinate, and can never expect to be the equal of white men . . ., I'll do what I can to help them. . . . But when they want to reverse nature, and rule white men, and marry white women, and sit in my parlor, then, by God! we'll hold them under if we have to lynch every Nigger in the land.
>
> (p. 176)

After he concludes his tirade, the judge says "John, the question is, are you, with your education and Northern notions, going to accept the situation and teach the darkies to be faithful servants and laborers as your fathers were." John accepts the frustration of living behind the Veil and keeping his Black neighbors behind their veil by responding, "I am going to accept the situation, Judge Henderson" (p. 176).

The stories I heard when I was young and the story "Of the Coming of John" (Du Bois, 1903) taught about the "color line" (veil and Veil) and the many ways it operates to oppress Blacks. When I thought about the curriculum I was given during my schooling and the counseling I received when I was in high school, it was to make certain that the "education and Northern notions" that I was hearing at home would be kept in check.

In 1909, Du Bois spoke on his paper "Evolution of the Race Problem" and argued strongly against the White supremacist discourses of the social Darwinists, nativists, and eugenicists that were rampant in society at that time. "Evolution of Race" is one of Du Bois's essays that I wished I had discovered during my college years; it would have been helpful in my arguments against the color line that operates through biased IQ testing and Arthur Jensen's 1969 article, "How Much Can We boost IQ and Scholastic Achievement?" White supremacists argued that race was a biological construct and that Blacks were of inferior stock and limited in attainment by nature. Such a statement based on flawed science caused Du Bois to ask, "Why is this?" and then to challenge the work of Darwin, Weissman, Galton, and others. Du Bois contended no consideration was given by these scientists to Blacks' decades in enslavement, receiving poor or no schooling since and during Emancipation, or Blacks being forced to live in poor conditions. As such, Du Bois argued, "Scientific claims that Blacks are inferior are based upon unscientific reasoning" (p. 3), and he further noted "the assumption [of Black inferiority and White superiority] is an outrageous falsehood dictated by selfishness, cowardice and greed" (p. 12).

In 1900, the Pan-African Conference was convened in London to "examine the situation facing the African race in every corner of the globe, to solemnly protest the unjust contempt and odious treatment which are still heaped upon the race everywhere" (Pambazuka News, 2016). Pan-Africanist values and ideas had emerged in the late 1800s in response to European colonization and exploitation of the African continent. Pan-Africanist philosophy argued that enslavement and colonialism were dependent on and encouraged negative and unscientific categorizations of race, culture, and values of African people. W. E. B. Du Bois and Anna Julia Cooper, from the United States, were invited to present papers at the first Pan-African Conference. Cooper spoke on the "The Negro Problem in America." Per archival sources, her speech has been lost. However, much of Cooper's scholarship addressed sexism and racism, and their intersections with social class and labor, education, democracy, and citizenship in America and countries abroad. Du Bois joined Cooper's focus on race in America, but at the Pan-African Conference, he expanded the idea of the color line into a global analysis and critique. Du Bois's use of the phrase "color line" and his explanation of the concept captured attention worldwide. Fredrick Douglas had previously used the phrase in 1883 in an article titled "The Color Line in America," and Du Bois had previously worked through and presented the crux of his Pan-African Conference speech, including his use of the words "color line" at the third annual meeting of the American Negro Academy earlier in 1900, titled "The Present Outlook for the Dark Races of Mankind." Du Bois (1900) told the Academy that he was going to consider "the problem of the color line, not simply as a national and personal question, but rather in its larger world aspect in time and space" (p. 1). Continuing with his address to the Academy, Du Bois (1900) added, "The secret of social progress is a wide and thorough understanding of the social forces which move and modify your age" (p. 2). However, it was during his address to the "Nations of the World" in 1900 that Du Bois rearticulated and clarified his statement on the "color line." In the fifth sentence of his address, Du Bois (1900) gave voice to humankind's problem statement when he explained,

> The problem of the twentieth century is the problem of the color-line, the question of how far differences of race—which show themselves chiefly in the color of skin and the texture of the hair—will hereafter be made the basis of denying to over half the world the right of sharing to their utmost ability the opportunities and privileges of modern civilization.
>
> (p. 1)

Next, Du Bois appealed to European leaders to grant colonies in Africa and the West Indies the right of self-government and for the United States to grant political and social rights to African Americans. The urgency of Du Bois's (1900) plea was because England, France, Germany, Spain, Holland, Belgium, and Portugal had carved out territories in Africa for themselves, and the United States was remaining silent as those countries colonized African countries. President Woodrow Wilson, who was president at the time, was a committed segregationist. As president of Princeton University, Wilson excluded Black students from living in the dormitories. As president of the United States, Wilson had separated federal civil servants by race and placed Black employees behind partitions, and he had given little attention to Africa in the formation of the League of Nations. Wilson's actions initiated a call to action by Blacks throughout the world. Du Bois argued that Europe was grabbing African land and that it must be stopped. To halt Europe, Du Bois and others organized the Pan-African Conference in 1900 in London to bring about global solidarity and cooperation among the African states to fight against colonialism and systematic racism.

"The Present Outlook for the Dark Races of Mankind" (Du Bois, 1900) became a teachable moment for me. I observed Du Bois evolve to become an international crusader against White supremacy. I saw how the thinking of a scholar progresses and how Du Bois expanded his idea to make the "color line" argument applicable in different locations. Race, racial domination, and exploitation are laid out as black skin color is inferior, white skin is superior and the humanity of people of color across the globe is equal to Whites. Du Bois, I saw, spoke to the problem when he said,

> My life had its significance and its only deep significance because it was part of a Problem; but that problem was, as I continue to think, the central problem of the world's democracies and so the Problem of the future world.
>
> (Du Bois, 1940, p. vii–viii)

I first learned about the racial problems and issues in Africa not from my school textbooks but from sitting in church and in my community. During Sunday church services, I heard references to White supremacists' discourses and exploitation of Blacks in Africa and the United States, as well as the neglect of the United States toward Africa. Some Sundays when I attended the eleven o'clock service with my mother, I would hear Reverend Austin at Pilgrim Baptist church speak about the suffering of Blacks in Africa, and he would take up a special collection for them. Politician and noted preacher, Congressman Adam Clayton Powell Jr., actor and singer Paul Robeson, and other Black celebrities who were recognized as "race men" also worked to inform Blacks in the United States about Pan-Africanism. They argued against the social Darwinists' ideology taking place in Africa. Robeson's films, *Song of Freedom* and *Jericho/Dark Sands*, were the first films that I saw that showed Africans in a positive light and showed their humanity as equal to the humanity of Whites. Robeson's movies stood in stark contrast to the Tarzan movies my friends and I were accustomed to seeing. In Roberson's movies, Africans were treated with respect and dignity. Africa was not only lions, jungles, and "great white hunters." Roberson's films showed the beauty and blemishes, success and failure of African countries and African people. African people, my friends and I learned, were like people of other races. This was a welcoming surprise to us, because we rarely saw Blacks in Africa portrayed as intelligent beings. That said, we never missed a Tarzan movie. Today, when my friends and I gather and look back, we ask ourselves, "Why did we drink the Kool-Aide?" In Tarzan movies—49 of which were made from 1918 to 2016—Blacks were portrayed as subhuman; the movies relied on racial stereotypes and social Darwinism. African natives were portrayed as ignorant, uncivilized, and easily overwhelmed by stronger and more powerful White capitalists and imperialists. Tarzan, the White savior, would kill or jail the White intruders, who were stealing ivory and minerals out of Africa. Tarzan's assistance in combating the evildoers usually came not from African natives, but from African animals with whom Tarzan had the unique ability to communicate.

My friends and I observed and contributed to such unscientific and socially constructed categorizations whenever we attended Tarzan movies. These destructive beliefs aided and promoted the rise of social Darwinism, eugenicism, and nativism. In 2014, when singer and civil rights activist Harry Belafonte received an honorary Oscar, he spoke about how Tarzan movies affected many young Black youth. The arguments he gave showed why Du Bois's Pan-African initiative was so important. Belafonte (2014) stated,

> In 1935, at the age of 8, sitting in a Harlem theater, I watched with awe and wonder incredible feats of the white superhero, Tarzan of the Apes. Tarzan was a sight to see. This porcelain Adonis, this white liberator, who could speak no language, swinging from tree to tree, saving Africa from the tragedy of destruction by a black indigenous population of inept, ignorant, void-of-any-skills, governed by ancient superstitions with no heart for Christian charity. Through this film the virus of racial inferiority—of never wanting to be identified with anything African—swept into the psyche of its youthful observers. And for the years that followed, Hollywood brought abundant opportunity for black children in their Harlem theaters to cheer Tarzan and boo Africans.
>
> (Quoted in Anderson, 2014, p. 2)

During the late 1970s and throughout the 1980s, I would pass Trinity United Church of Christ on 95th Street in Chicago on the way to visit my brother Shelby. In 1978, I noticed a sign that said, "Free South Africa." When I asked my brother, a founding member of the Trinity, about the sign, he told me that Reverend Jeremiah Wright Jr., the pastor of the church, had placed it there. Shelby said that the sign would remain until Nelson Mandela was released from prison. Every time I passed the sign, my thoughts would rush back to Du Bois and Cooper and their work opposing the color line at the

Pan-African Conference. In 1990, Mandela was freed, and the sign was removed from Trinity's lawn. When I first recognized that the sign was down, I thought not only of Mandela but also of a long struggle of Pan-Africanism that began in the late 1800s and Du Bois's (1900) "To the Nation of the World" speech.

Sustainability and Resilience in Bronzeville

The development of Bronzeville announced to the White governing authority at city hall in Chicago that Black migrants from the South were there to stay; the color line would not turn them away, nor would they succumb to White authority. Throughout his work, Du Bois addressed the progress of Blacks and the path they should take to sustain their being and make known their humanity. From reading Du Bois's (1903) essays "Of Mr. Booker T. Washington and Others" and "Of Our Spiritual Striving," I learned about his philosophy on assisting Blacks to move forward. Du Bois argued that Blacks should not engage in adjustment and submission. As a teacher, my reading of Du Bois suggested that I should seek to empower my students and their communities. Du Bois's contribution to my everyday life and later my research encouraged me to listen to multiple voices, use multiple lens, and critique White power. I believed these ideas were important to preparing the next generation of Blacks to not be dismayed by the color line and to remain resilient. Philosophically, Du Bois's efforts were focused on establishing the equality of Blacks. While doing so, Du Bois (1903) supported the history of all races and peoples. Du Bois contended that for Blacks to sustain their being, they had to build Bronzeville, Harlem, and other Black communities.

A theme that ran through Du Bois's work is "truth," and "truth" I came to understand was the motivation for my work. Initially, I wanted to point out to my students the lies, distortions, and omissions in their curriculum material that I realized from my reading of Du Bois, Woodson, Cooper, and others. Du Bois had and believed he had "a fuller view of truth" than others (Byerman, 1994, p. 7). "Truth" for Du Bois developed from, and the relentless search for it was motivated by, his fight for racial equality and the promotion of understanding between people. Du Bois's dissertation, *The Suppression of the African Slave Trade to the United States of America, 1638–1870*, at Harvard, and his first book, *The Philadelphia Negro*, were efforts to provide "truth" to Whites about their flawed thinking and understanding about Blacks based on scientific sociological data. Du Bois wanted, I learned, to use "truth" to build bridges with Whites, not to scold them, but to first point out falsities and to use that information to get Whites to self-correct. Du Bois also contended that truth and rightness are "unseparated and inseparable." Du Bois (1926) opined, not out of arrogance, but as a statement of "truth" to Whites that reflected his "confidence in his grasp of truth" (Byerman, 1994, p. 7) that "I am one who tells the truth and exposes evil and seeks with Beauty and for Beauty to set the world right." Du Bois (1926) argued the apostle of truth and right are bounded by truth and justice. Du Bois imagined "Beauty," as moral justice, functioning to set the world right. "The apostle of Beauty, thus becomes the apostle of Truth and Right, not by choice but by inner and outer compulsion" (Du Bois, 1926, p. 1). "Right," Du Bois contended, is the agent of political and social change, and is the necessary complement to beauty and truth.

Thus, I asked myself, How can a teacher tell Black children the story they are about to read is "beautiful" in text and picture, and about their humanity if Black history and culture are featured stereotypically or secondarily, or not included on the reading list? "Goodness," Du Bois (1926) states, "is in all its aspects of justice, honor and right—not for sake of an ethical sanction, but as the one true method of gaining sympathy and human interest." (p. 24). Although "Truth," "Rightness," and "Beauty" are supposedly core values in American society, including in the schoolhouse, they often are absent in the treatment of Blacks and the education of Black children. Keith Byerman (1994), reflecting on Du Bois and "truth," provides a comment about Du Bois's imagining of "Truth" that is relevant to young Blacks speaking truth to power and struggling through youth movements and protest in the United States and globally to get the general population of people to eliminate corrupt authority and reinstitute democratic fair play. Byerman (1994) contends that Du Bois saw "truth" as a "Law of the Father," which "challenges the corrupt father . . . The son, by supplanting the father can install an 'empire' of reason, morality, and beauty to replace arbitrary power and self-interest" (p. 7, 8).

Du Bois argued that for Blacks to sustain their being and bring about racial equality, they needed to have well-equipped colleges and universities, a firm belief in their ability to excel, and a desire to work hard. In addition, Du Bois argued that Blacks should not allow the "Negro problem" that was created by Whites to be shifted to the shoulders of Blacks as Whites stand aside as critical pessimistic spectators. The numerous stories I heard as a child told of how Whites would place blame on Blacks in order to save face for the slightest of things that sometimes led to Blacks being punished.

As an educator, most of Du Bois's philosophical and practical ideas on education to help Blacks toward racial equality and full recognition of their full humanity were useful to my

teaching and research. Du Bois believed education was a powerful weapon that could be used to resist White supremacy
and bring about the empowerment of Blacks. However, Du
Bois also knew that education, when it is denied or when it is
absent of "Truth," lacking in "Beauty," and does not support
what is "Right," only serves those who oppress. I concur with
Provenzo's (2002) thesis that Du Bois believed "that education
was a two-edged sword, which could be used to either to liberate or subjugate specific social and cultural groups" (p. 4).

Places of Episodic Memory

The South Side Community Art Center, George Cleveland
Hall Library, and the YMCA at 3763 S. Wabash were the places
where I consciously and unconsciously engaged with Du Bois's
ideas and work. In some cases when I engaged with his ideas
and work, I was unaware at the time that they would shape my
ideas later in life.

South Side Community Art Center (SSCAC)

When I entered high school and was permitted to travel about
Bronzeville, one of the places my friends and I visited was
the SSCAC. We did so not because we had a thirst for literary knowledge or were driven by a desire to become artists
or to attend workshops or classes, rather we did it to be cool.
The SSCAC was a "happening place." First Lady Eleanor Roo-
sevelt had attended the grand opening, which was broadcast
across the country on CBS radio. It was a place with a rich
and deep history and sense of community. Also, we knew girls
from all over of the south side of Chicago came to SSCAC.
Unbeknownst to me at the time, I was discovering one of the

places in Bronzeville where the genres of art and scholarship that would come to play a significant role in my scholarship and leisure were developing.

The SSCAC was a space where the young fathers and mothers of urban realism, who argued for portraying the realities of Black life, gathered. There were soon to be iconic Black artists and writers, such as Richard Wright, Gwendolyn Brooks, Willard Motley, and Margaret Goss Burroughs. Richard Wright (1937), who is credited with the leadership of Black artists in Chicago, stated,

> For the Negro writer to depict this new reality—black life with its beauty marks and blemishes—requires a greater discipline and consciousness than was necessary for the so-called Harlem school of expression . . . . The relationship between reality and the artistic image is not always direct and simple.
>
> (p. 11)

Echoing themes from Du Bois's work, Wright (1937) addressed the importance of unity between the races when he stated, "On the shoulders of white writers and Negro writers alike rest the responsibility of ending . . . mistrust and isolation" (p. 11). Wright (1937) wanted Black artists to believe in themselves, to lift the "veil," and to come out of the Veil and see themselves through their own eyes and not through the eyes of White people. Wright (1937) posits,

> When Negro writers think they have arrived at something which smacks of truth, humanity, they should want to test it with others, feel it with a degree of passion and strength that will enable them to communicate it to millions who are groping like themselves.
>
> (p. 11)

Wright had picked up on Du Bois's argument for Blacks to encourage critiques from one another to strengthen their understanding and develop clarity so that all Blacks moved forward together. Du Bois made this point in his disagreement with Fredrick Douglass, who was a friend and mentor. Du Bois, upon assuming Douglass's mantle of Black leadership after his death, argued against Douglass's assimilationist and amalgamationist point of view. In the "Conservation of the Races," Du Bois (1897) rejects amalgamation and makes the case for the creation and conservation of a distinct Black identity and community. Du Bois states,

> It may, however, be objected here that the situation of our race in America renders this attitude impossible; that our sole hope of salvation lies in our being able to lose our race identity in the commingled blood of the nation; and that any other course would merely increase the friction of races which we call race prejudice, and against which we have so long and so earnestly fought.
>
> (p. 2)

Chicago writers examined life in the city, collaborated with sociologists and leftist radicals, and looked toward to a better future. "The art was a collection of moderate and radical versions of African American history and visions for racial progress," as well as an examination of the Black consciousness. The literary genius of Richard Wright (*Black Boy*, *Native Son*), the scholarship of Horace Clayton and St. Clair Drake (*Black Metropolis: A Study of Negro life in a Northern City*), the intellectual creativity of Langston Hughes ("The Negro Speaks of Rivers," "The Negro Artist and the Racial Mountain"), and the inspirational and realistic verses of Gwendolyn Brooks ("We Real Cool," "Kitchenette Building"), among others were what I was awaking to. Soaking up the cultural realism about Black life, I had no idea at the time that I would later research and write about it, nor did I realize I was living in the moment when Black intellectual thought on urban realism was born. That knowledge would come later. Lines from Gwendolyn Brooks's (1963), "Kitchenette Building" poetically described the realism of urban life. In the cramped one-room apartments where Black families lived, the kitchenettes were where many breakfasts, lunches, and dinners were cooked on hot plates.

Both Du Bois and Alain Locke, leaders of the Harlem Renaissance, worked to build an upscale Black cultural identity. *The New Negro* came to respect and to appreciate the art of urban realism. Locke, considered by many the dean of the Harlem Renaissance, commenting about how the artists of urban realism documented explicitly the horrible realities of life for Black people in America stated,

> More and more you will notice in their canvasses the sober realism which goes beneath the jazzy, superficial show of things or the more picturesqueness of the Negro to the deeper truths of life, even the social problems of religion, labor, housing, lynching, unemployment, and the likes. For today's beauty, must not be pretty with sentiment but solid and dignified with truth.
>
> (Locke as quoted in Jeffrey Helgeson, 2012, p. 129)

Visiting the SSCAC taught me about the way artists portrayed the humanity of Blacks, their condition and station in life, and the problems and issues that came with living within the veil and the work that would be necessary for Black people to come permanently out of the Veil. It was the narrative of equality and justice that Du Bois wrote about and advocated.

It was the stories I was hearing on my front porch when the adults gathered, expressed in a different medium. The artists of SSCAC stood on the shoulders of Du Bois; the "color line," "veil/Veil," "double consciousness," and "democracy," as well as the sustainability and resilience of Black humanity, were prominent in the work I saw. As contemporaries of Drake and Cayton (1945), SSAC artists' work depicted Negro life in Chicago. In *The Black Metropolis*, Drake and Cayton (1945) drew on Du Bois's "color line" to frame their argument. Drake and Cayton (1945) commenting on the color line stated:

> At first glance this seems like a very narrow, ethnocentric approach to world affairs . . . [however] . . . European powers has been based upon . . . subordination of the colored peoples of Asia and Africa . . . The color-line is America is merely a specialized variant of this worldwide problem.
>
> (p. 97)

At the opening and dedication of the SSCAC, in 1940, Margaret Burroughs said,

> We believed that the purpose of art was to record the times. As young black artists, we looked around and recorded in our various media what we saw. It was not our imagination that we painted slums and ghettos, or sad, hollow-eyed black men and women and children. They were the people around us. We were part of them. They were us.
>
> (Burroughs as quoted in Schlaback, 2013, p. 117)

Growing up in Chicago, I admired the work of those who, like Richard Wright, wrote about the race, gender, and class realities of urban life for Blacks in Chicago in the 1930s and 1940s.

Whereas I appreciated the work of Du Bois and others who wrote about race, class, and gender of the Harlem Renaissance and the *New Negro*, I had a bias toward the urban realism of Chicago. However, my admiration for the work of both Du Bois and Wright led to searching out connections between Du Bois and Wright and my work. Bobby Wilson's (2002) article "Critically Understanding Race-Connected Practices: A Reading of W. E. B. Du Bois and Richard Wright" was helpful in making the three-way connection. Wilson (2002) argued that Du Bois's and Wright's work on race-connected practices/racism should be examined in both a historical and geographical context. Borrowing from Lefebvre (1991), who contends "groups, classes, ideas, values, and political systems produce their space at particular historical moments," Wilson (2002) points out how both scholars came to contextualize history and geography. My studies of schooling use both geography, urban Chicago, and history, my childhood/youth and Chicago school closings in 2014, to study race, class, and gender. My research that draws on the work of both Du Bois and Wright has benefited from their inclusion of geography and history in their work.

Two years ago, while visiting Chicago, I stopped by the SSCAC with a good buddy with whom I used to go there. The center looked smaller than I remembered, but the art of urban realism featuring both a historical and geographical slant still abounded. Silently, the scholarship of Du Bois and Wright abounded. My friend and I reminisced with the director about our time there, and I promised the director I would come back and give a talk on a book I had recently completed. As my buddy and I descended the stairs, we passed three young men of high school age coming up. My buddy and I smiled at one another; we had a hunch about why they were there.

Hopefully, their visit would be as life sustaining as our visits had been.

George Cleveland Hall Library

In 1932, the George Cleveland Hall Library, a branch of the Chicago Public Library, was constructed in Bronzeville. Hall Library was another place where the influence of Du Bois's work affected me, though here, too, the influence was not direct. Vivian Gordon Harsh, the first African American branch librarian in the Chicago Public Library system developed a "Special Negro Collection." The Hall Library rapidly became a place to foster and locate the historic and current cultural and literary works of Black Americans. Harsh's appointment and the development of the Negro Collection received a favorable response from Blacks locally and nationally. Material on Black history and culture were donated in abundance. The George Cleveland Hall Library quickly became a favorite place in Bronzeville, because it was a place where Blacks could learn their history in a supportive environment. People shared opinions, told stories, and recommended writings to one another. Blacks felt at home. Hall Library nurtured the work of Black students, scholars, and writers. When the president of the Chicago Library's board of directors discovered that the library was usually filled to capacity with Black people learning about their history and culture, and reading Du Bois, Wright, and others, he became concerned. He argued that it might lead to a race riot.

Although Chicago was the home of urban realism, Black Chicagoans also wanted to read the work of Du Bois. He was known and respected. Harsh, in a telegram to Du Bois, recognized him as the "Dean of Writers." Harsh (1948) writes,

Dr. W. E. B. Du Bois:

It is with admiration and reverence that we greet you whose life is a challenge to heirs of American culture at Hall Branch Library. We feel especially honored to send this message to the Dean of Writers whose Great literary works we are privileged to handle daily.

Best wishes, Vivian G. Harsh and Staff

My late brother, Ernest, first introduced me to the Hall Library and the Special Collection. He was the one who told me about Vivian Harsh. Ernest and I, as the youngest two of my mother's four sons, did many things together. However, one summer day when I came in from outside, I asked my mother, "Where's Ernest?" Mother told me he had gone to the library on 46th and Michigan—the Hall Branch. Usually, when Ernest and I would go to the library, it was the main public library downtown on Randolph and Michigan, where I would poke around stuff on science and Ernest would head to the historical section. A few hours later, Ernest returned home carrying a shopping bag with 13 books. Thirteen books to read. I thought Ernest had lost his mind. "Ernest . . . what are you going to do with all of those books?" Ernest looked at me and said. "Read them. . . . Isn't that what you do with books?"

Later that day, Ernest told me that he had heard about Hall Library from the librarian at school. Throughout high school, Ernest continued his trek to Hall Library. I saw the names of Du Bois, Douglass, and others who contributed to Black intellectual thought. I recall wondering how "Du Bois" was pronounced and asking Ernest. He sighed and told me, taking his time to make sure I got it, while letting me know, although he was the younger brother, I was on his turf. Some years later, when I read *Souls* for the first time, the opening statement in the forethought of the book made me think of Ernest and his discovery when he visited the "Special Collection." Du Bois (1903a) writes,

> Herein lie buried many things which if read with patience may show the strange meaning of being black here in the dawning of the twentieth century. This meaning is not without interest to you, gentle reader; for the problem of the twentieth century is the problem of the color-line.

(p. 3)

By visiting Hall Library, Ernest was receiving an education about the ideologies and mythologies of racism and Black history and culture that was not offered at our school. Students like me, who were pursuing a different discipline, were being educated to ignore; that is the way the Chicago Public School (CPS) school system was planned and designed.

In 2013, I was invited to the George Cleveland Hall Library to deliver a lecture with my brother Shelby on *The Moment: Barack Obama, Jeremiah Wright and the Firestorm at Trinity United Church of Christ* (Grant and Grant, 2012), which had been recently published. I had been to Hall Library a few times after Ernest began going, but this time as I arrived at the library with Shelby, my thoughts were not on the lecture we were going to deliver; my thoughts were on Ernest, who had recently died. I was about to speak in a special space—a room where notables such as Richard Wright, Langston Hughes, Zora Neale Hurston, Arna Bontemps, Gwendolyn Brooks, Horace Cayton, William Attaway, Margaret Walker, Alain Locke, and St. Clair Drake had spoken. I was in a library where the scholarship of Woodson and the "Dean of Writers," Du Bois was prized and celebrated, and their works eagerly read by young and old. But more importantly to me, I was in Ernest's space. The chairs, tables, and lectern were vintage, and the dates on the black-and-white photos of Black icons I mentioned earlier hung in the room that I knew Ernest had visited and enjoyed many times. While we were being introduced, discussions, I had with Ernest flowed through my mind. I thought about how he had pronounced "Du Bois" for me and many other discussions we had had about the Hall Library. I knew if Ernest had been there, he would have smiled or offered his distinctive laugh and congratulated me on being in *his space* and doing the work I am doing. Ernest would have said to me, "Dude, I was the one who really introduced you to Du Bois, Woodson, Cooper, and all those other people you are now writing and teaching about. I didn't invite you before, because I didn't think you were ready. Now you are ready . . . I think. . . . Don't screw this up!"

In *Souls*, Du Bois (1903a) reminds us of what Ernest understood and believed: "We have no right to sit silently by while the inevitable seeds are sown for a harvest of disaster to our children, black and white" (p. 28). These words from Du Bois were meaningful to me and other scholars of color who met at the National Association for Multicultural Education conference a few days after the 2016 presidential election. Our voices were filled with passion and energy about a task placed before us because of the results of the election. We see disaster facing the youth of America and are determined not to let it happen.

Wabash YMCA

The Wabash YMCA was a place my friends and I regularly attended to play basketball, swim, and enjoy Friday night dances. Now a Chicago landmark, it was built in 1913. The "Y," as many in the community referred to it, was an important part of community life in Bronzeville. During the Great Migration, its 102 rooms provided housing for Blacks with no relatives and friends in the city and little money. It offered job training and tutorials about how to apply for a job. The Y's large assembly hall was used to host many educational and social programs. It was used to teach migrants about Black history and culture, and introduced Black migrants to city life to ease their transition into the Black Belt.

In 1915, it was the founding site of the Association for the Study of Negro Life and History, now called the Association for the Study of African American Life and History (ASALH), by Carter G. Woodson. Woodson went on to found the *Journal of Negro History* in 1916, to orchestrate the founding of Negro History Week in 1926, and to publish the *Miseducation of the Negro* in 1933. The works of Woodson, Du Bois, and other Black notables received attention at the "Y." Posters and notices of lectures, workshops, and poetry readings on Black history and culture could not be missed by those of us attending the "Y" to engage in sports activities or dances. When I asked my friend Bob when and where he first recalls hearing of Du Bois, Bob quipped, "Not in school! It was at the Wabash Y. I saw a picture of Du Bois shaking the hand of Walter Worrill." Worrill was the activist program director at the Y and the cofounder of the Task Force for Black Political Empowerment.

One day, when speaking with Timuel Black, a noted historian on Bronzeville, he told me that he had spoken to men who were in the audience when Woodson announced the founding of ASALH at the "Y" and of their excitement. Timuel and I spoke of the development of Black history and culture in in Bronzeville. I learned of Du Bois's speech, "The Criteria of Negro Art," delivered in Chicago in 1926 at the conference for the NAACP. Du Bois's speech was in honor of Carter G. Woodson receiving the twelfth Spingarn Medal. During the speech, Du Bois (1926) argued against the "*art for art's sake*" thesis. Du Bois stated,

> All Art is propaganda . . . and whatever art I have for writing has been used always for propaganda for gaining the rights of black folks to love and enjoy, I do not care a damn for any art that is not used for propaganda. But I do care when propaganda is confined to one side while the other is stripped and silent.
>
> (p. 253)

Du Bois's words resonated me with on a personal and professional level. I realized my writing—my art—is for "propaganda." Before reading Du Bois's "The Criteria of Negro Art," I had always associated propaganda with what false messaging combatants do to one another to mislead. After reading Du Bois's essay, I looked over my research, writing, and speaking—all of it is "propaganda" for the racial equality for Black children and other children of color. Before stopping to think about Du Bois's words, an acceptance letter from an editor about an article or book that I had written was a step forward on the tenure path or a plus for my merit review. Afterward, I saw my work as propaganda attacking the inferiority of Black students and demanding that their humanity be fully respected. When I look about my home, each piece of art hanging or standing in it is propaganda for social justice or speaks to the humanity of all people.

The politicization of art in Du Bois's address lent itself to the construction of a distinctly Black cultural milieu, free from the pressure of having to please a White audience and White patrons that want Blacks portrayed in stereotypical images. And, although Du Bois's "The Criteria of Negro Art" stirred up debate among Black artists over whether the work of the Black artists should be for social and political goals of racial equality or for its own aesthetic purpose, it was a debate that I contended needed to take place among a developing people, who were 50 plus years from enslavement and determining their own direction. The debate serves as a teaching moment to explain to Black youth, those who are in doubt about the fullness of their humanity, how, in the 1920s, Black people were making their own choices about the nature of the culture they would leave for them. Additionally, after reading Du Bois's essay, it clarified for me the confusion I'd had during my youth as I traveled through Bronzeville partly listening but not asking questions about the "equality or aesthetic" questions that were unclear to me.

Du Bois understood the controversy he had raised with the speech honoring Woodson, and he was aware of the plight of the poor Black artists. In 1925, in the "Social Origins of the Negro Art," Du Bois argued, "As the Negro rises more and more toward economic freedom, he is going on the one hand to say more clearly what he wants to say and do and realize what the ends and methods of expression may be." (p. 240). Du Bois's words are meaningful because, although at the time he was discouraged that Black progress was moving so slowly, and angry at the intervention by Whites to curtail the progress, he nevertheless held a profound belief in a successful future of Black people equal to all other people once they were economically and politically free. Additionally, Du Bois's "Social Origin" statement helps me to understand that although both Du Bois and Locke advocated the Black aesthetic tradition of African or folk art, and they wanted to turn the page on text and pictures of enslavement and bring on the *New Negro*, they knew that Black people who had control of their lives would create art to tell the story they wanted told. Richard Wright (1937) exemplified this idea when he called for a new theory of African American writing, where the writer does not work to determine him/herself against the literary models of a White public, but to carve out his/her own aesthetic in representing lived experience. Lastly, Du Bois's statement of "propaganda" is one that remains with me daily, especially when I visit schools and other public spaces, and observe the signs, symbol, icons, and heroes and heroines visually displayed. I look to see what messages they are sending to Blacks, people of color, and Whites. Controlling messaging and branding is important in the struggle for full equality.

Smarter Today Than Yesterday

Concluding Chapter 1 and moving on to Chapter 2 causes me to look backward as I move forward. It suggests an occasion when Du Bois looked back, assessed the here and now, and then offered an enlightenment that he would take forward. The time was 1953, shortly before *Brown v. Board of Education*. Du Bois was celebrating the fifth anniversary of *Souls*. When he took a moment to reassess, perhaps the most well-known and quoted statement in *Souls*, "The problem of the twentieth century, is the problem of the color-line," Du Bois said,

> I still think today as yesterday the color line is a problem of this century. But today, I see more clearly than yesterday that back of the problem of race and color lies a greater problem and that is the fact that so many civilized persons are willing to live in comfort even if the price of this is poverty, ignorance, and disease of the majority of their fellow men; that to maintain these privileges men have waged war until today war tends to become universal and continuous, and the excuse for this war continues to be color and race.
>
> (Du Bois, 1957, quoted in Davidson, 2007, p. 207)

Looking backward and considering racial progress since 1953, when Du Bois made his reassessment, I too see the color line as a problem. And I too see that too many people are willing to live in comfort, even if the price of this is poverty, ignorance, and neglect for most of their fellow human beings. The neoliberal, individualistic, and meritocratic moment we are in provides peace of mind for some civilized persons to live in comfort and privilege with little regard for how poverty and injustice are affecting many citizens. In Chapter 2 of *Du Bois and Education*, I discuss the color line and its impact on my work as a CPS teacher and administrator, as well as my graduate schooling. During these undertakings, I learned more about Du Bois and had a great need for his ideas and vision.

References

Belafonte, H. (2014). Quoted in Anderson, B. (2014). Harry Belafonte Names Tarzan as Hollywood's most racist super villain. Available online: http://downtrend.com/71superb/harry-belafonte-names-tarzan-as-hollywoods-most-racist-super-villain.

Beyerman, K. E. (1994). *Seizing the word: History, art, and self in the work of W. E. B. Bois.* Athens, GA: University of Georgia Press.

Brooks, G. (1963). Kitchenette Building. *Poetry Foundation.* Available online: www.poetryfoundation.org/resources/learning/core-poems/detail/43308 (accessed 7 May 2017).

Davidson, O. G. (2007). *The best of enemies: Race and redemption in the new South.* Chapel Hill, NC: University of North Carolina Press.

Douglas, F. (1883). The Color Line in America. Black History. Available online: http://academic.eb.com/blackhistory/article-9399839.

Drake, S. C. and Cayton, H. (1945). *Black metropolis: A study of Negro life in a northern city.* New York: Harcourt, Brace and Co.

Du Bois, W. E. B. (1897). The Conservation of the Races. Teaching American History.org. Available online: hingamericanhistory.org/library/document/the-conservation-of-races/ (accessed 3 May 2017).

Du Bois, W. E. B. (1900). To the Nations of the World. BlackPast.org. Available online: www.blackpast.org/1900-w-e-b-du-bois-nations-world.

Du Bois, W. E. B. (1903a/1994a). *The souls of black folk*. New York: Dover.

Du Bois, W. E. B. (1903b). The Talented Tenth. Available online: http://teachingamericanhistory.org/library/document/the-talented-tenth/.

Du Bois, W. E. B. (1909). The Evolution of the Race Problem. Available online: www.webdubois.org/dbEvolOfRaceProb.html.

Du Bois, W. E. B. (1917). The Migration of Negroes. *The Crisis*, June, 63–66.

Du Bois, W. E. B. (1920). The Social Equality of Whites and Blacks. *The Crisis*, 21, November, 1920, 16.

Du Bois, W. E. B. (1925). *Darkwater: Voices from within the veil*. New York: Harcourt, Brace and Howe.

Du Bois, W. E. B. (1925). The Social Origins of American Negro. http://credo.library.umass.edu/view/full/mums312-b208-i033. 3/20/17.

Du Bois, W. E. B. (1926). Criteria of Negro Art. *The Crisis*, October, 290–297.

Du Bois, W. E. B. (1937). "The nucleus of class consciousness." Pittsburgh Courier. In. Du Bois, W. E. B. The world of W. E. B: A Sourcebook. Santa Barbara, CA: Greenwood.

Du Bois, W. E. B. (1940). Dusk of Dawn. Oxford: Oxford University Press.

Du Bois, W. E. B. (1944). My evolving program for Negro Education. In Rayford W. Logan (Ed.), *What the negro wants*. Chapel Hill, NC: The University of North Carolina Press.

Du Bois, W. E. B. (1957). Quoted in Osha Gray Davidson (2007). *The best of enemies: Race and redemption in the new south*. Chapel Hill, SC: The University of North Carolina Press.

Du Bois, W. E. B. (1970). Criteria for Negro Art. In W. E. B. Du Bois & W. Meyer (Eds.), *W. E. B. Du Bois: A reader* (p. 253). New York: Harper & Row. The article was first published in *The Crisis* in 1926, and was originally a speech delivered to the Chicago Conference of the National Advancement of Colored People W. E. B. Du Bois (1909).

Du Bois, W. E. B. (2014). *John Brown* (The Oxford W. E. B. Du Bois). Edited by Henry Louis Gates, Jr. Oxford: Oxford University Press.

Gates, L. G. Jr. (n.d.). Who Really Invented the 'Talented Tenth'? The African Americans. www.pbs.org/wnet/african-americans-many-rivers-to-cross/history/who-really-invented-the-talented-tenth/. Accessed 4/12/17.

Grant, C. A. and Grant, S. J. (2012). *The moment: Barack Obama, Jeremiah Wright, and the firestorm at Trinity United Church of Christ*. Lanham, MD: Rowman and Littlefield.

Harsh, V. (1948). Telegram from Chicago Public Library to W. E. B. Du Bois. www.digitalcommonwealth.org/search/commonwealth-oai:9s166 g9ox. 3/19/17.

Helgeson, J. (2012). Who are you America but me? In D. C. Hine & J. McCluskey (Eds.), *The Black Chicago Renaissance* (pp. 126–146). Urbana, IL: University Illinois Press.

Hughes, L., Rampersad, A., & MacLaren, J. (2001). *The collected works of Langston Hughes, vol. 13: The collected works of Langston Hughes.* Columbia, MO: University of Missouri Press.

James, J. (1997). Transcending the Talented Tenth: Black Leaders and American Intellectuals. Available online: www.hartford-hwp.com/archives/45a/426.html (accessed 6 January 2016).

King, L'Monique (2013). The relevance and redefining of Du Bois's talented tenth: Two centuries later, *Papers & Publications: Interdisciplinary Journal of Undergraduate Research*, vol. 2, Article 9.

Lefebvre, H. (1991). *The production of space.* Maiden, Mass: Blackwell.

Pambazuka News (November 17, 2016). Pan-Africanism in Our Time. Available online: www.pambazuka.org/pan-africanism/pan-africanism-our-time. (accessed 4 January 2017).

Provenzo, E. F. (2002). *Du Bois on education.* Lanham, NJ: AltaMira Press.

Sawyer, M. (n. d.). The Duboisian V[v]eil{s} Reexamined. Available online: www.academia.edu/4793595/The_Duboisian_V_v_eil_s_Reexamined (accessed 4 April 2016).

Schlaback, E. (2013). *Along the streets of Bronzeville.* Urbana, IL: University of Illinois Press.

Tulving, E. (1972). Episodic and semantic memory. In E. Tulving & W. Donaldson (Eds.), *Organization of memory* (pp. 381–403). New York: Academic Press.

Wells, I. B. (1892). Editorial. Free speech and headlight weekly. In Alfreda M. Duster (Ed.), *Crusade for justice: The autobiography of Ida B. Wells* (1970). Chicago: University of Chicago Press.

Wilson, B. M. (2002). "Critically Understanding Race-Connected Practices: A Reading of W. E. B. DuBois and Richard Wright." *The Professional Geographer*, 54(1), 31–41.

Wright, R. (1937). *12 million black voices.* New York: Basic Books.

2

THE COLOR LINE AT WORK AND IN GRADUATE SCHOOL

My life had its significance and its only deep significance because it was part of a Problem.

(Du Bois, 1940, p. vii–viii)

In Chapter 2, the days of my youth are behind me, and I am out of the Bronzeville bubble. My story of *Du Bois and Education* continues with some discussion of my undergraduate days, where I was formally and passionately introduced to Du Bois. I use quotations from Du Bois as section headings, and I am surprised, but pleased, by how well most of them work. Most of the chapter centers on my time as a teacher, assistant principle, and graduate student. I relive critical moments in these experiences, along with including Du Boisian observations to show his relevance to these educational experiences. The "color line/veil/Veil," "problem," "stirring," "propaganda,"

and other ideas that Du Bois used in the struggle for racial
equality and Black humanity are included. I begin with a
life-changing invitation from a friend.

Bob's Invitation, Changed My Life

"Believe in life! Always Human Beings Will Progress to Greater,
Broader, and Fuller Life."

(Du Bois, 1957/1963)

*"Bob is your car outside? Does it have gas? If so let's get the hell
out of here!"* It was a Monday after a Friday that was payday.
When I arrived at the Sommers Elementary where I was working, the school secretary immediately informed me that 14
teachers were out. Some substitute teachers were on the way,
but not enough to cover 14 classes. The school principal was
at a district meeting, and as the assistant principal in charge
of order and control, the staff looked to me to deal with the
problem of approximately 550 students arriving to teacherless
rooms in 45 minutes.

It was about eleven o'clock when I headed to the school
office to announce that all was good when I heard a famil-
iar voice calling. "Carl." I tuned to greet the voice that I knew
from my middle school years. I turned and asked, "Bob, what
are you doing here?" Bob told me, that he was at the school to
work with the three guidance counselors. Bob's professional
specialty was school counseling and guidance. His current
focus was providing staff development for White school guidance counselors working with Black students.

Bob and I had grown up together. We were more than
school buddies; we were good friends, along with Lornie and
our other friend Bob. After quickly catching up, Bob issued an
invitation to me that changed my life. "Carl," he said, "come up

the University of Wisconsin-Madison and work on your PhD." Bob told me he was taking courses at UW in the Department of Curriculum and Instruction (C&I).

"Wisconsin," I interrupted. "Isn't that about a two-and-a-half to three-hour drive?"

Bob replied, "Yes. I leave Chicago at about two p.m. twice a week to meet a four thirty class." Bob then said, "Carl, I know you are planning to get a PhD. Come to Madison. I think you will like it. I can set up a meeting for you with my advisor, John Antes."

Later, Bob told me he met John when he was working on his master's at Oberlin College in Ohio. Bob explained that he attended Oberlin for three years during the summer to earn a master's degree in counseling and guidance. He said after John accepted a position as professor at UW in C & I, he encouraged Bob to enroll. Bob's invitation hung in the air. As I stared at him, my mind was racing. I had already concluded that the CPS's efforts to deal with structural racism in the school system were weak to nonexistent. Ben Willis, the CPS superintendent, had a policy and practice of resisting or compromising on efforts to desegregate the schools. He did very little to support quality education for Black children, who were becoming the majority as Whites fled to the suburbs. In addition, Willis snubbed Dr. Martin Luther King Jr. when he came to Chicago to facilitate meetings between CPS and the Black community about the city's segregated, poverty-ridden schools. I took Willis's snub of King personally. Willis had snubbed me and every Black person in Chicago.

When King was in Chicago, his place for meetings and preaching was Liberty Baptist Church on the south side of Chicago at 4848 S. Parkway Drive (which changed to Dr. Martin Luther King Jr. Drive in 1968, the year King was assassinated). Liberty was my mother's church. One Sunday, when I accompanied Mother to church, King's sermon addressed city hall and CPS's resistance to eliminating school and housing desegregation. King spoke of Willis's and Mayor Daley's resistance to school desegregation and encouraged Blacks not to give in, but to "keep their eyes on the prize." Listening to King take words and phrases like "racial injustice" and "desegregation" and put a face on them as he described a catalogue of dehumanization and humiliation that Blacks in Chicago were dealing with, I felt inspired to be more proactive against racism, regardless of the consequences. His comments about Willis and Daley were not mean-spirited, but he preached of two men who had lost sight of their Christian values.

In a Du Boisian sense, King's speeches were oral propaganda for racial equality and Black humanity, and Du Bois's writings were prose or written propaganda for racial equality and Black humanity. Also, both King and Du Bois informed my theorizing, lecturing, and storytelling with their different styles of messaging. King's words were inspirational. He brought them to life by making them characters who played out a dramatic episode about social equality. Du Bois provided a more academic analysis and discourse to challenge systemic racism; in doing so, he placed Whites' insatiable desire and demand for privilege in historical and contemporary contexts. Both Du Bois and King helped me to have a deeper understanding and appreciation of my role and responsibility as a teacher of Black children working against the color line.

The Color Line at Work: "Education must not simply teach work—it must teach life."

(Du Bois, 1903b)

Harry Belafonte recalls a moment midway through the Civil Rights Movement when Martin Luther King Jr., appearing agitated and preoccupied, stated,

> I've come upon something that disturbs me deeply. . . . We have fought hard and long for integration, as I believe we should have, and I know that we will win. But I've come to believe we're integrating into a burning house.

I have thought about this a lot and wonder when does one discover that they are "integrating Black students into a burning house?"

Like many Blacks, after the passage of *Brown* and the civil rights legislation of the 1960s, I cautiously hoped that never again would any citizen be denied access to education, jobs, voting, travel, public accommodations, or housing because of their race. As a teacher of Black children, my thoughts were on preparing students so they could live a flourishing life, be morally good citizens, and have the highest regard for the humanity of others.

My first assigned classroom after subbing in Chicago for several months was at Wadsworth, a K–8 school on the southeast side of Chicago that was dealing with a rapid increase of Black students. The Wadsworth faculty was a mixture of experienced and first- and second-year teachers. Most of the new teachers were Black. During my first year, I became known among my colleagues as the teacher who told Mr. Pearl, the principal, that the science textbooks were racially biased, and I didn't plan to use them. It was my first experience pushing back on the color line as a professional. Hearing my statement, Mr. Pearl said, "Mr. Grant, you know science, so tell your students what they need to know." I know the expression on my face told Mr. Pearl what I thought of his racialized comment, so I turned and walked away. Initially, I thought Mr. Pearl would send me packing with a "who does this first-year teacher, no tenure, and an unknown within the teachers' union think he is?" Instead, later in the year, he appointed me as the Wadsworth school representative to the district textbook selection committee.

As a teacher at Wadsworth, my goal was to get students academically and socially ready for their futures, which I hoped would be an integrated society. I stayed late to tutor, to listen to my students' problems, and to help them with their schoolwork. I wanted to build rapport, which was essential to my teaching method. I understood I was teaching students and not a subject.

I wanted to help my students become aware of America's history of denying Blacks equality. Twelve- to 14-year-old Black children, and even younger, are abundantly aware of structural racism. I wanted them to know how their history had been stolen, distorted, and omitted from the America story. I told them to ask their grandparents to tell them about why their family members wanted to come to the North and ask them to discuss their hopes and dreams as they were traveling. I asked them to please look into the faces of the person telling the stories and to read the emotions they saw. I asked them not to always ask their grandparents or other Black elders to bake a cake or pie for them, but to tell them about their own personal stories and their hopes for them and their other family members. Spontaneously, as much as planned, when a teachable moment appeared, I told historical stories of Black-led breakthroughs in science and medicine, as well as deaths in service to America and names with racial identities that should be included in person killed in the Boston

Massacre, was Black; that George Washington Carver, the bot-
anist and chemist who revolutionized the use of peanut was
Black, or that Dr. Daniel Williams who performed the first
successful American open-heart surgery at Provident Hospital in Chicago, a hospital that Dr. Williams had founded and
one of the few hospitals in Chicago that welcomed African
Americans, was also Black (African American Registry, 2013).
The CPS curriculum, I explained to students, did not include
such information because CPS did not want Blacks knowing
that they are contributors to society.

I taught eighth grade science in a team-teaching arrange-
ment with four other teachers: Jenkins, art and music; Davis,
English; Newberry, mathematics; and Wilson, social studies. I
was a firm believer that "science," like no other subject, could
excite academic and social learning. The Teaching Team con-
centrated on the academic learning and social awareness that
our students needed to reach their career goals. We wanted
students not only to prepare for high school and college
but also to prepare themselves so well that they would have
a choice in the college they would attend. We preached, "In
this 'new day' in America, leaving school after four years of
high school is a no, no! "Your grandparents left school after
high school because social conditions limited the number of
colleges they could attend, money for college tuition was difficult to come by, and the acceptance rate of Black students
was low." We argued, "Today is not your grandparents' day. It
is your day! Keep your eyes on the prize. Don't submit to the
color line." We wanted students to understand the significance
of education and its importance to them, their families, their
race, and the rest of humanity.

Most of our students didn't have a family member who had
attended college and few were considering college. We wanted a

major change in their thinking about college. We talked a good deal about ourselves to let them know that their teachers had been in their position not too long ago. We drew on the goals and language of the Civil Rights Movement because it was an inspirational experience and an event in our students' and their parents' lives. To the Team, the curriculum consisted of the national and local ideas and events going on and ongoing. We integrated current events around the Civil Rights Movement and Black History—their intersection—into the teaching of mathematics, history, music, reading, writing, and art prescribed by CPS. We taught with an energy that demanded 110% from our students, and our students responded and accepted our academic and social challenges. Students faced down their academic challenges and to a person engaged in the grit of learning. Discipline problems rapidly came under control and then became nonexistent. Human problems—no lunch money, concern about food for the weekend—received careful, quiet attention.

We got to know the parents of each of our homeroom students by sitting in their homes and listening to them tell us about their expectations for their child and letting them know that we were there for them. Those efforts were a part of our push against our students' and their parents' feelings of inferiority, and we encouraged both not to judge themselves through the lens of White people or their inability to find employment, but to be themselves and to keep striving. Du Bois's (1903a) statement, "To attain his place in the world, he must be himself, and not another" (p. 4), is what the Teaching Team was working to convey to both students and parents.

We were five young Black teachers with little teaching experience, but with a good deal of passion and reasons for wanting change. We explained that we were not there to save them;

they didn't need saving. They needed fair treatment and a bit of support from people who cared and saw them as equal. We were dedicated to making a difference.

> The ruling of men is the effort to direct the individual actions of many persons toward some end. This end theoretically should be the greatest good of all, but no human group has ever reached this ideal because of ignorance and selfishness.
>
> (Du Bois, 1920, p. 78)

Most days, the Teaching Team, as we called ourselves, ate lunch together. It was during our meals together that our doubts would seep out. We questioned the possibilities of King's dream ever becoming reality. On the national level, we were aware that school desegregation was barely creeping, far from crawling. The Supreme Court order, "with all deliberate speed," instead of "forthwith" to achieve racial desegregation had become not only a doctrine to delay compliance with *Brown* but also an attitude among many Whites to resist or proceed very slowly with desegregation. In response to the resistance to desegregation and superficial integration, it became a part of the Teaching Team's "official curriculum" for some students or teachers to give an update on the progress of the Civil Rights Movement and/or to discuss resistance to the Civil Rights Movement during homeroom meetings. Governor of Alabama George Wallace's 1963 statement, "I draw the line in the dust and toss the gauntlet, before the feet of tyranny and I say segregation now, segregation tomorrow, segregation forever," served as our foundational rallying call.

Wilson, my late good buddy who traveled up to Madison to attend football games with me, would remind us that it was very difficult, if not impossible, for full civil rights to be achieved:

"They [Whites] screwed us during and after Emancipation and they screwed us after we fought and died in World War I and II, to save the homeland of their grandparents." Wilson would continue, explaining why the color line was difficult to transverse, especially on those days when he read about some protesters being injured, or worse, carrying out their First Amendment rights.

> If we didn't remain in the back of the bus, they [Whites] would argue we were arrogant "Ns." As soldiers, they didn't want to fight next to us. Do you think they have changed or want to change? Hell, no!

Wilson's analysis was accurate. He was verbally exercising the frustration and anger that Du Bois (1903a) did when he wrote that the history of the American Negro is one of strife and longing to have their humanity accepted. The Black person, Du Bois contended, "simply wishes to make it possible for a man to be both a Negro and an American, without being cursed and spit upon by his fellows, without having the doors of Opportunity closed roughly in his face" (p. 11).

It was in moments like those that we faced reality: unbounded White supremacy and privilege to prevent Black children from having a positive identity of themselves. I would ask myself, "Will there ever be a way forward toward complete elimination of the color line and complete equality so Blacks are no longer subjected to live behind the veil or within the Veil?" Moments of reality also heighten our determination to prepare our students to teach them about the veil/color line. We explained that living behind the veil/color line structures that Whites set up consciously and unconsciously clouds Blacks' capabilities to see their true selves. This is so, we explained, because the veil is literally a barrier (e.g., White supremacists' ideology, policy, practice, and privilege) placed in front of Blacks to halt their progress literally, thereby causing Blacks to doubt themselves, to have a "double consciousness, and not have true self-consciousness. Du Bois (1903a) notes, I explained, that the "gift" of the second-sight/double consciousness/"racialized knowledge" does not yield true self-consciousness. In addition, we wanted our students to understand that their parents and teachers wanted them to achieve to their fullest academic or vocational potential and that they should strive to do so with all their might. That said, they heard from us, at that moment in time, even with goals achieved, that they would have to live within the Veil. That was because Whites do not accept Blacks as equals, despite their educational achievements being equal. However, we hoped to lift the Veil for my students so that "we darker souls might peer through to other worlds," as Du Bois's teachers at Fisk did for him (Du Bois, 1920, p. 8).

We also pointed out with examples that even if the "dream" was delayed, there would be more opportunities than previously existed. Blacks and other like-minded people had taken sufficient action to bring about some changes. Protests and agitations were having some positive effects. Also, as part of their preparation, one, sometimes two, Saturday mornings each month, one or two of the Teaching Team would take between 15–25 students downtown to visit museums and art galleries, and dine in restaurants that offered a different cuisine and setting than they would find in the Wadsworth community.

The Teaching Team understood, as Du Bois (1903a) did, that "education is that whole system of human training within and without the school house walls, which molds and develops men [sic]" (p. 11). Our Saturday excursions were a part of preparing students for entering spaces where they had little experience. However, we worked not to reinscribe the superiority of Whiteness. We taught the students about Black art and culture. Because art (writ large) by Blacks and other people of color was not as readily available in the downtown galleries, we visited sites with a Black heritage. We explained the history of the social growth and development of the Chicago Black Belt where they lived. We spoke of Bronzeville as an artistic and cultural project that was built despite the structural racism from Chicago City Hall's efforts to control its growth. The South Side Community Center, the 37th Street YMCA, the Hall Library, and the Michael Reese Hospital on the south side of Chicago were places we highlighted. We argued against the narrative that Black things are not as good as White things: a White doctor or lawyer is not smarter than a Black doctor or lawyer. We pointed out that although the city's "founding fathers" didn't recognize the efforts of Blacks in the city center, Blacks were contributors to the history and culture of Chicago, starting with Jean Baptiste Point du Sable. We told them the story of Point du Sable, the Black man who was the founder of Chicago in the late 1770s. We discussed how the city's fathers, through exercising White supremacy and privilege over decades, did not acknowledge, or marginalized, the Black founder of the city.

The Teaching Team wanted the students to do as Du Bois would come to do after his card was rejected by the White girl new at his school: to move forward with a passion and purpose.

Davis, Wilson, Newberry, and I were attending graduate school in the evening. We each were pursuing a master's degree in education at different Chicago universities. When we discussed our course work, we learned that the texts and journal articles we were assigned to read and what we were hearing from professors' lectures was pretty much the same: Schools in urban areas are failures. Black children are responsible for their lack of achievement. They have a cultural deficit. The deficit rationality was supported in two national reports. The first was the Moynihan Report in 1965 titled *The Negro Family: The Case for National Action*. It was a controversial report that argued, "The single-parent mother-headed family (e.g., family structure) in the urban areas was becoming increasingly common, and the high percent of out-of-wedlock birthrate, more so, than the legacy of enslavement was causing Blacks' social conditions." Although Du Bois (1899) raised hard questions about poverty, crime, and illiteracy in Black homes in *The Philadelphia Negro* and Franklin Frazier (1939) raised questions in the *Negro Family in the United States*, both argued that the root cause of Blacks' social condition was the legacy of enslavement and little support after Emancipation and during Reconstruction. However, although Moynihan recognized enslavement, he argued that Blacks were caught up in a "triangle of pathology" (unemployment, education failure, fatherlessness, and criminality) brought on less by the legacy of enslavement and more so by single-parent homes.

The second report, the Coleman Report of 1966, titled *Equality of Opportunity*, claimed that family background contributes to disparities in children's school performance (Viadero, 2006) and in doing so gave academic creditability to the cultural deficit thesis. Countless academic journal articles, dissertations, and master's theses were written, and lectures and speeches given at education conferences across the globe, positing the social and intellectual deficit of Black children. Black children as culturally deficit became the topic of conversation during the lunch hour in many schools, and Black children as objects of research became the preferred focus for articles in scholarly journals. The two national reports and much of the research that followed aided in keeping Blacks behind the color line/ veil and kept in place Blacks' feelings that their chance for a successful social and economic life was dubious. These feelings highlighted "this sense of always . . . measuring one's souls by the tape of a world that looks on in amused contempt and pity" writes Du Bois (1903a, p. 11).

> Children learn more from what you are than what you teach.
>
> (Du Bois, 1898, p. 18)

To this day, I wonder about the interview that moved me from classroom teacher to assistant principal. The year was 1967. It was a typical school day; I was teaching science to a group of eighth graders when a student entered my room with a note from the office. "Mr. Pearl would like you to come to his office, ASAP." I told my students I needed to run down to the office for a few minutes and to continue with their work; I would be back in a flash. I darted out of my room, running down the stairs wondering, "What in the heck is this all about?" Mr. Pearl and I were on good terms (as far as I knew); he had placed me on a district-wide textbook selection committee after I told him the science textbook assigned to me was sans people of color who had contributed to the field to science.

My curiosity didn't last long, because in less than 60 seconds, I was standing before the school clerk. She pointed to the principal's office door and said, "Go in, Mr. Grant." I tapped lightly on the door and heard, "Come in." It was my very first time in Mr. Pearl's office, although I had been working at Wadsworth for about five years. Mr. Pearl was White, thirtysomething, stocky, and, according to him, a good athlete in his youth. He was seated behind a desk that was too small for him, but necessary for the little office space. The interior of his office was pretty much like him: plain and simple in décor. The only visible personal effects were a picture of his wife, Deidter, and him, and a picture of his three children. I had met Deidter at a school holiday party. She was charming and taught fifth grade at a suburban school. Seated in a chair next to Mr. Pearl's desk was a tall White man in his late fifties or early sixties, dressed in a washed-out, wrinkled gray suit, a light-blue shirt, and a dark-blue tie. We were introduced to one another. I was not asked to sit down and join the discussion. I was told the other man, Mr. Grift, was the principal of Sommers on the Westside. I was asked *one* question: "Are you interested in becoming an assistant principal?"

"Yes," I replied. I was told I could return to my class.

I walked slowly back up to my class, asking myself, "What, just happened?" Friends of mine who had completed applications to become an assistant principal were interviewed extensively. Some said a few questions had bordered too close to the personal. When my friends and I were sharing interview information with one another, we would laugh about the personal questions saying, "The White man wants *all* details about the Black people he is hiring," In Du Bois's (1926) "Criteria of Negro Art," the essay I referenced in Chapter 1, Du Bois discusses "interpretations" that come about when "new stirrings" are occurring in the Black community. Blacks, of course, as any humans, have different reactions and interpretations to new opportunities and events and how they are portrayed. Whites, because they are White, also have interpretations and suggestions about "new stirrings" that go on in the Black community. For illustration, the Harlem Renaissance brought about a "new stirring" over the development of "Negro Art." As Blacks discussed among themselves the direction of *their* art, White's wanted in on the discussion. Whites wanted Negro art to maintain the status quo of Blackness and Whiteness and to serve White self-interests and their conception of Blacks because such art would be easier to sell to other Whites.

I soon discovered that my hiring and promotion to assistant principal was not about helping the education of Black children but about serving the interest of Whites. The "new stirring" from the Civil Rights Movement and the increase of Black families on the south and west sides of Chicago, moving into areas that for years had been occupied by Whites, caused challenges and disruptions to Whites who only wanted to live in all-White communities. As the long-held racist real estate code of "no Blacks" began to crack, White families immediately ran to the suburbs. In doing so, they left behind schools with no White students for the many White teachers and other White staff members assigned to those schools. CPS had too many White teachers to transfer to White schools on the north side of Chicago. White teachers, many of them young and inexperienced, felt trapped and afraid. They had never planned to teach Black children. Their reasons for wanting to teach because they "love children" and "want to help children" did not apply to Black children. The plan, with all the earmarks of being hatched in the upper office of CPS, was to place a Black in each school as assistant principal in charge of order and control.

On the Thursday of the following week, I received a call from the CPS district office telling me to report to Sommers Elementary the following Monday morning as an assistant principal. I had one day to say good-bye to my Teaching Team, other teachers and staff, colleagues and my students.

Mr. Pearl came up to my room the next day (Friday afternoon), shook my hand, and said, "You will be an excellent assistant principal, Mr. Grant. Good luck." He told the students that they would have a new teacher Monday morning and left. That was it! My students were extremely sad and several cried. I felt pangs of guilt, and I was sad about leaving and frustrated about the way I was leaving. There was no time for a transition with students and my replacement. My Teacher Team, however, saw my leaving as a "success" in our struggle to improve the overall education for Black children in Chicago. I was simply moving on to help bring about the changes the Civil Rights Movement was struggling to achieve: to help Blacks behind the veil. I had proven teaching ideas from the Team to take with me. The Teaching Team, including myself, didn't realize that often when Blacks are promoted, it is first to serve the self-interest of Whites. Du Bois (1903a) correctly noted that the relationship between Whites and Blacks had always been essentially one of domination, exploitation, and narrow opportunity, so why should I have expected anything to be different.

The next morning, Saturday, I drove over to Sommers Elementary. From the outside, it was a well-cared-for school: no broken windows, grass recently cut, and no trash and clutter around the building. Then I saw the 30 Willis Wagons on the school's playground. "Wow! I said to myself. Willis Wagons were a visible, in-your-face demonstration of "domination, exploitation, and narrow opportunity" because they "celled" Black children ages six to eight. A Willis Wagon was a term coined by the Woodlawn Organization to describe the portable aluminum 20 x 36 foot school classrooms placed on school grounds by CPS Superintendent Benjamin C. Willis so that his racist school administration would not have to allow Black children to attend White schools, although there were plenty of empty seats and some schools were only a short distance away. Willis believed that White self-interest and privilege was more important than racial equality and a quality education for Black children. The Willis Wagon, thus, became a major source of tension—the color line—between the Black community and CPS.

As I toured the community that Saturday morning, I chatted with neighborhood kids, visited the small mom-and-pop, nickel-and-dime store a block from the school. I introduced myself to the owners, a man and women. I walked a half mile each way—north, south, east, and west—from the school. I wanted to see the school's community; I wanted to see where students lived: the houses, apartment buildings, streets and intersections, parks, churches, businesses, and supermarkets. I wanted to learn if there was a Boys and Girls Club or a YMCA; there was not. Knowing the community helped me identify the resources available for the children, including businesses that could be helpful in financing school projects as well as helping families in critical times. I viewed this as basic knowledge for my job. As I walked about the school community, I introduced myself as the new person at the school who wanted to help. I asked people I met to give me an opportunity and to let others in the community know that I was available. I let Black parents know that I came to listen and learn. I told them, "I am a good listener; talk to me." To some in the neighborhood and at the school, my actions were strange. School leaders and teachers were not out in the community connecting with students' families and community members. Family members came to the school; the school didn't go to them. In *The Philadelphia Negro* (Du Bois, 1899), Du Bois's study of Blacks who lived in the 7th Ward of Philadelphia, Du Bois learned that Blacks didn't like being objects in studies. I tried to avoid this difficulty by listening, not taking notes, and being friendly.

Merl Eppse, one of my professors at TSU, was a big admirer of Du Bois. In the two classes I took with him, I received a steady diet of Du Bois's ideas and thoughts. Eppse had come to know Du Bois because he was embarrassed that he didn't know of his work when his White political science professor asked, "Eppse, who is Du Bois?" In the forward of his book, Eppse (1943) writes, "I did not give him a satisfactory answer. This was the beginning of my interest in my own people" (p. 1).

In canvassing the Sommers Elementary School community, I was doing what I had been taught by Du Bois and Eppse: to learn about a people, you must go out among them, visit where they go, spend time in the places where they are, talk with them, and give them the opportunity to know you and come to trust you. In his early work, including *The Philadelphia Negro* and when he taught at Wilberforce, Du Bois was critical of himself for not knowing his people. Du Bois (1899) wrote,

> The colored people of Philadelphia . . . had a natural dislike for being studied like a strange species. . . . I concluded I didn't know so much as I might about my own people, and when. . . . [I was] invited to Atlanta University . . . to teach sociology and study the Negro, I accepted.
>
> (p. 11)

The following Monday morning, after my Saturday walking tour, I arrived at Sommers a bit anxious, but confident. My walking tour had been helpful in providing insights into the school and staff, and although I was concern about my role of mainly serving the interests of Whites, I walked through the

entrance door dedicated to keeping up the "stirring" and striving to help Black students as much as possible.

How does it feel to be a problem?

(Du Bois, 1903a, p. 1)

All my friends and I appreciated our advancement in CPS, but
we didn't lie to ourselves about the extent to which we were
influencing racist policies and a school system that gave little
care and attention to Black students. There were many stories my Black assistant principal colleagues would tell about
noble deeds done to help Black children each day and that was
good for the children we helped. However, my Black assistant
principal colleagues and I knew we were a "Band-Aid for a
gunshot wound." Our main responsibility was to prevent
Black children, especially boys, from giving White teachers a
problem—a problem often socially constructed out of racial
bias, inexperience, and ineptness. There was little thought
given to the idea that White teachers were major contributors
to their own classroom problems. Our next responsibility was
to deal with the growing enrollment of Black students and
parents who were new to the school and community.

In 1903, Du Bois raised the powerful question, "How does
it feel to be a problem?" (p. 1). Arguably, few, if any, of the
Black students at the school knew of W. E. B. Du Bois. But like
Du Bois, Black students wondered aloud why they were always
signaled out as the problem. From the first day they enroll in
school, many Black boys have a similar issue to the one Du Bois
experienced as a student: being a "problem"—a problem created by the enslavement of Blacks by Whites and their refusal
to eliminate racism from America after Emancipation. During
my conferences with Black students, they described feeling

that they were not being acknowledged as ordinary students. Several boys were constantly put down by teachers and made to become the class joke. Becoming a class joke led to other Black children in the class piling on. The Black children who laughed and went along with the teacher did not understand that they were buying into a White authority figure oppressing one of their own and that they were, therefore oppressing themselves. When I explained this to the "go along students," it did not take them long to understand what I was telling them.

Too often, the curiosity and mischief of a seven-year-old Black boy was interpreted as a "disorder" that needed to be controlled with medication. Almost never did Mr. Grift want to hear that the real problem was that the teacher could not teach and held bias about Black children. Here I am not using "teach" as a synonym for "discipline." Literally, several teachers could not teach. They had major difficulties with mathematics and science content knowledge, and pedagogical content knowledge, and they had poor pedagogical teaching habits and practices. The situation was difficult for me, in part because my options to improve it were very limited. I knew the Administrative Team (principal and three assistants) would flat-out reject releasing the teachers in part because they were fixated on blaming Black children. A major theme in Du Bois's scholarship was what I experienced with the Administrative Team: the Negro as a problem to Whites. Du Bois searched to understand what it meant to be an educated Black person among White people who only perceive Blacks and other people of color as trouble and as a drag on the well-being of the nation. I learned after a few weeks with the Administrative Team that my best option to help students who were perceived as a problem was to place Black boys in a Black teacher's class. Objections to this idea were almost nonexistent. The Black boy—the problem—was removed from upsetting the White teacher, and it had been suggested by the Black assistant principal. The White Administrative Team members' hands were clean and the problem was solved! Moments such as these were filled with displays of White power and privilege at a high cost to Blacks. The poor quality of teaching that Black children were receiving could influence the way they thought about their ability to learn and their self-worth. The Black students have to measure their academic ability by the tape of poor teaching. I say, borrowing Du Bois's (1903a) words, "How hard a thing is life to the lowly, and yet how human and real!" (p. 45).

My Black assistant principal friends and I were given very little opportunity and no authority to change the school curriculum and practices in ways that would better welcome and make the school day more exciting and academically fulfilling for Black children. Sommers was the color line in educational guises. "Truth," "Beauty," and "Right" were on an extended holiday. Upon entry into Sommers' office, Black parents were greeted by pictures and artifacts of White ethnics who no longer attended the school. Signs, symbols, and images of persons of color were not present in the school office. Every face that looked up from the work at their desks to greet a Black parent was a cultural mismatch, and people in need of human relations training, but who had not received it. There was not in symbols, signs, or human voice a "Welcome. This too is your school. Teachers and staff will help you to prepare your child to achieve their career goals." The school's "propaganda" in signs and symbols were stating this is a school that is used to welcoming White students only. Ironically, the last White student at the school had transferred out more than three years before I arrived. Nevertheless, their ghosts remained throughout the building. Pictures of graduation ceremonies from previous decades and White personalities dominated the library and other public areas. The mark of "Whiteness" was the "propaganda" everywhere.

The efforts of Black parents to keep alive the curiosity and joy their young child had less than an hour before, when they bounced out of their homes heading to Sommers for the first time, was on the threshold of being lost. Those young Black students had not entered a friendly and welcoming environment. Du Bois (1903a) echoed the sad reality that dejected Black parents encountered at school when he remarked, "The history of the American Negro is the history of ... strife." (p. 3).

There were 28 White teachers at the school; many of them had never been in close spaces with Black children and youth. There were 15 African American teachers. There were also two other assistant principals, both of whom were White women. The first, Ms. Richards, had more than three decades at the school and was responsible for p/K–3. Ms. Richard's responsibilities included overseeing the Head Start Program and 30 Willis Wagons of first to third graders. Ms. Kusso, the second assistant principal, was responsible for grades 4–6. She had worked at Sommers for 15 years. She always followed Ms. Richards's lead and discussed changes in policy and practice based on Richards's suggestions. I was responsible for grades 7–8 and the discipline of all children. Also, I was the faculty/administrator representative to the PTA and any other functions where Black parents or community members were involved, including responding to questions about the placement of children in Willis Wagons, although, technically, that was Ms. Richards's turf. To the frequent inquiries about the placement of young Black children in Willis Wagons, I asked parents and community members to consider the work the Woodlawn Organization was doing on the behalf of the African American community in regard to the

Willis Wagons. I refused to spout the official line that "they are new, safe, air-conditioned, self-sustaining units with toilets and running water."

The Willis Wagons were void of windows at eye level for children in the primary grades to look out and see the sky, sun, or birds. There was little room to skip to the pencil sharpener; there was only enough space to enter and take a seat along with 25–30 other students and remain fenced in until recess. The young Black children in the cramped Willis Wagon would in a few years learn that they were not treated as well as their White peers on the north side. They would soon come to understand that this was so because the Mayor's Office and Ben Willis saw them as not worthy of an excellent education. They believed their only obligation to Black children was to meet minimum state requirements. "America is not another word for Opportunity for all her sons [and daughters]" noted Du Bois (1903a, p. 88).

During the late 1960s, Sam Greenlee published *The Spook Who Sat by the Door*, a story about a Central Intelligence Agency (CIA) officer (a spook). The "spook" was the first African American agent hired by the CIA. The African American spook attended meetings and events to show that the CIA was committed to racial integration and social progress, but the spook had no power; he was only a showpiece for the agency. Often, when I attended community meetings to represent the school, I felt like the spook. I had no power. I was a showpiece. For any discussion that required an "OK" from the school, I would say, "I will propose this idea or that idea at our Administrative Team meeting." I was free to move about in the Veil; however, I understood that to my two White assistant principal colleagues and the White principal, my Black body demanded that I be held in check in order to maintain White interest.

As assistant principal in charge of the eighth grade graduation program, Ms. Richards and Ms. Kusso quizzed me during Administrative Team meetings on what I was planning to do as Mr. Graf looked on in silent approval of their quizzing. They begin to coach me about the ritual and routine of the graduation ceremony at the school.

"Whatever, you decide to do, go slow with any [cultural] changes." Their approach to keep me in line was under the guise of helping me because I was new to preparing graduation. "New stirring" (Du Bois, 1926, p. 2) by Black people, as I discussed in Chapter 1, led to Richards and Kusso conniving to maintain White interest and supremacy. As I sat and listened, pretending to take notes to reduce my comments to them, I felt as Du Bois (1903a) stated, "Being a problem is a strange experience,—peculiar even for one who has never been anything else" (p. 1). Du Bois didn't respond to his White colleagues/friends who asked him the question, "How does it feel to be a problem?" because he "would not bleach his Negro soul in a flood of white Americanism" (Du Bois, p. 2). I remained silent too. I understood that any and everything I said would be interpreted through a White frame of how a graduation ceremony should be carried out: music, speeches, and so forth. Instead, I decided not to "bleach Black culture in a flood of White prejudice and racism" (Du Bois, 1903a). As I listened, my intention grew stronger to carry out the graduation ceremony in a way that would make the Black graduates and their parents proud with cultural pride. I would kick the color line and then accept the consequences. "He simply wishes to make it possible for a man to be both a Negro and an American, without being cursed and spit upon by his fellows, without having the doors of Opportunity closed roughly in his face" (Du Bois, 1903a, p. 2).

Sommers didn't outwardly adopt a school theme that promoted the Civils Right Movement. The movement and King's efforts in Chicago to end segregated schools was big in the minds and hearts of Blacks in the community, and contributed to the reasons the community members disliked the school principal and disliked coming to the school. Arguably, the absence of attention to the Civil Rights Movement made it easier for teachers to adhere directly to CPS curriculum guidelines and the teaching suggestions in textbooks. The CPS curriculum guides, textbooks, and other curriculum materials were antiseptic in their approach to race and racism. As one of the three assistant principals at the school, my duties, especially as chief disciplinarian, allowed me to observe teachers teaching under the pretense of observing Black students' classroom behavior. In many teachers' classrooms, I would have never known that our country was engaging in a civil rights struggle that was of major significance to Black students and the Black community. The posters on the walls and books available for students to read when they finished assignments were "propaganda" (Du Bois, 1926) that promoted the White status quo and that largely ignored the events of the 1960s. What Black children were seeing on television in the evening was cast as having little to no relevance to their education at school.

Several of the newer teachers who consider their teaching style "progressive" adapted a color-blind ideology and chose not to look deeply into how race shapes the thoughts and actions of the American society, including their own actions. New code words and phrases became a part of teachers' vocabulary, such as "single-parent family" and "culturally deprived." Many of the White teachers, and some of the Black teachers, bought into the "propaganda" of culturally deficit rhetoric about Black children from their university textbooks written by White authors. They taught their classes as if there were only a few students in attendance with the ability to attend college or learn technical skills. They taught using the thesis born during enslavement that Blacks are a material resource to perform low-skill jobs. Their education should be minimal because an "education that encourages aspiration, that sets the loftiest of ideals and seeks as an end culture and character rather than bread-winning, is the privilege of white men and the danger and delusion of black" (Du Bois, 1903a, p. 58).

On some days, both Black and White teachers and staff members allowed the circumstances or the events of the Civil Rights Movement to challenge their professionalism. Several Black teachers—who had grown up in the South, attended HBCUs, and for their first time in their lives were living in the North and working with Whites—didn't hold back emotions. They openly expressed their views on civil rights within the context of the negative experiences they had lived through. They were a new and different generation of Blacks from the friends and neighbors who sat on my porch when I was young. During my youth, we whispered among ourselves "Black is Beautiful," "Power to the people," and similar words to that effect. The new generation shouted "Black is Beautiful" unhesitatingly. They kicked and shouted at the color line. Similarly, several of the White teachers who had grown up in White communities and had lived a life of White privilege (McIntosh, 1989) didn't appreciate the attitude and comments of the Black teachers and pushed backed. There were times when the teachers' lounge was not the place to eat lunch or hang out during a short break, or it was the place to hear the new "propaganda" for Black humanity. This new generation of Black and some White teachers made up about 30% of the teacher corps at the school, and at times, the tension among these two groups would boil over. In the final paragraph of "The Souls of White Folk," Du Bois (1925) asks why White people hang on to fables of the past, and the answer he receives is one that reverberates through the world: because "I am White!" (p. 29).

In 1989, Peggy McIntosh wrote an illuminating essay that told of her privilege as a White woman. Du Bois's statements on "Whiteness" made decades before agreed with McIntosh's analysis of Whiteness. McIntosh described how she was taught to see herself as a person whose moral will depended on her individual moral will and that she thinks of her life as moral neutral and normative (p. 1). What McIntosh describes is what I saw with most of the White teachers and staff at Sommers: "Whiteness is the ownership of the earth forever and ever." (Du Bois, 1925, p. 18).

As I entered Sommers each morning, I, like Du Bois and King, was ever the optimist. That said, I cursed the displays of White power and privilege and always wondered what I could do that day to make it better for students. I was honest and straightforward with students about their education and behavior, as well as the amount of power and authority I had to help. I spoke to them about the importance of staying on task and self-discipline. I explained that I was aware of the micro-aggressions they received from some of the White staff. Nevertheless, I encouraged them to "keep on keeping on" and to be resilient, because they knew getting an education was a *must*. I told students I wished I could do more, but I couldn't come into their teachers' classrooms and fire them. I would always close my conversations with the students the same as I did with my children and now grandchildren: "You know I will be supportive in every way I can, but you must hang in there and do your part. To stop or not do your best is to surrender to racism."

Teaching at Wadsworth and serving as an assistant principal at Sommers was my sociological laboratory. I observed the knowledge, skills, and attitudes of Black and White teachers, administrators, and staff, teaching and carrying out the administration of education for Black children. I saw White privilege daily, up close and personal. I saw Black teachers who had not yet learned how to work with Black children because they were "mis-educated" (Woodson, 1933). I observed the "color line"—poor teaching, boring curriculum, uncaring administration; Willis Wagons; anti-Black "propaganda"; little to no acknowledge of the Civil Rights Movement in the school; few or no posters and pictures that represented the Black culture in the public area of the school; resistance to the "stirring" of the Black community; and absence of acknowledgment that Black students were the students at the school now. Also, I saw several Black teachers and a few White teachers who were totally committed to the education of Black children. They were angry and frustrated about what they saw—the poor teaching, superficial commitment, and ineffective curriculum—going on around them. Several Black teachers were further annoyed because when they raised their Veil and could look deeply into morass of the circumstances of Black students, especially Black boys, they saw that Black boys, in comparison to their White male peers on the north side of Chicago, would remain continuously marginalized and would probably be worse off throughout their lives. These Black teachers understood and agreed with Du Bois's (1903a) statement when he was writing about the life struggle of his mentor and friend Alexander Crummell:

> [The] . . . black boy finds it just a little harder; if it is difficult for you to find and face your duty, it is a shade more difficult for him; if your

> heart sickens in the blood and dust of battle, remember that to him
> the dust is thicker and the battle fiercer.
>
> (p. 139)

> Education is the development of power and ideal; The worker must
> work for the glory of his handiwork, not simply for pay; the thinker
> must think for truth, not fame.
>
> (Du Bois, 1903a, p. 54)

Bob and I didn't leave for Madison the morning he invited me to come to UW. A month later, however, on a beautiful Saturday in October, we arrived in Madison. I met John Antes, and we discussed education in the United States, particularly in the urban areas, and our life experiences and families. John, a Quaker, former US Air Force pilot, was a very decent and caring man. Two-and-one-half months later, in January 1969, I was a graduate student at UW. I drove back and forth from Chicago to Madison two days a week for 13 months to attend classes. The drive soon became boring flat land and tollbooths, and then Chicago's traffic, which is always heavy. And although it is probably a bit corny, I never saw the PhD as just for me: "The thinker must think for truth, not for fame."

A few months ago, I flew up to Minnesota for Bob's surprise birthday party. As the person at the party who had known Bob the longest, I was invited to give a toast and to share stories of our youth. I concluded my stories with a big thank you to Bob for inviting me join him in grad school at UW.

> For education among all kinds of men always has had, and always
> will have, an element of danger and revolution, of dissatisfaction
> and discontent.
>
> (Du Bois, 1903a, p. 20)

Early in 1971, my family and I moved to Madison. We settled in a brand-new housing complex: Monona Shores. Carl,
four; Alicia, a couple of months old; my wife, Gloria; and I
took the move and adjustment from Chicago in good spirits.
In fact, we enjoyed it. No more 45–55 minute drives on Chicago expressways to get to Sommers and then home each day.
Having a temporary relief from dealing with the daily realities
of life in a school was like a good soul food dinner.

Madison and the UW campus was struggling to climb out
of the Vietnam war protests and the civil rights protests that
had taken place on the campus. Gloria and I had followed
the student campus protests across the country at Berkley,
San Francisco State, Howard University, and on several other
campuses. We had discussed at length the Black student-led
strike for increased minority recruitment and retention, and
the establishment of an Afro American Department at UW,
as well as the response of Governor Knowles calling out the
National Guard on the UW campus.

Once again, I was witnessing "new stirrings" (Du Bois,
1926) by Blacks that were resisted by Whites. Knowles and
the university authorities asked the same questions Whites
asked when Blacks began "stirring": "What do you want?
Why are you not satisfied?" The response, by Black UW students was mostly the same as it has been for centuries: "We
want to be Americans, full-fledged Americans, with all the
rights of other American citizens" (Du Bois, 1926, p. 2). We
want to live on a campus where people want to learn about
other people—their history and culture—as well as math,
science, and traditional US history, where men and women
create scientific developments and knowledge for becoming
global citizens, and where each person's humanity is prized
and people help one another to enjoy life and to learn. It is

that sort of campus that we want to create for ourselves and for all UW students.

We saw reactions to the "stirrings" in our classes. Some professors were hesitant to engage in curriculum change and some had difficulty responding to questions that challenged Eurocentric framing and disagreements during discussions. The "stirring" of Black students to bring about a new appreciation of what America and the UW campus could be was met with racialized self-interest policies, weak compromises, delays, and resistance. Nevertheless, among Black students on campus, there was a new will to be. The struggle with the UW authorities was tough, but the students stood strong. The Black students had a legacy of strength. They were the sons and daughters of former enslaved persons or people who fought racism all their lives, Blacks who had fought and died in World War I and II on soil they nor their relatives ever called home, or on an ocean where members of their bloodline only knew about the waves of the oceans from below decks during the transatlantic slave trade.

Gloria, Bob, and I received numerous thoughtless and disguised racist queries and comments about how and why we came to choose UW since there were plenty of good universities in Chicago. We were asked if we were really pursuing PhDs or maybe we really meant to say MAs. Questions about the newly established Afro American Studies Department on campus were directed to us: "Shouldn't it be the responsibility of the Afro Studies Department and the University Wisconsin-Milwaukee to primarily teach about African American history and culture?" "Will there be White professors in the Afro Department?" "Can a White teach Black history in the Afro Department?" The queries we received, once again, reminded me of Du Bois's (1903a) statement about how his colleagues verbally "danced" about when asking him, "How does it feel to be a problem?" (p. 2). Gloria, Bob, and I, like Du Bois (1903a), decided not to say a word.

Madison was not the liberal town that the Chamber of Commerce liked to portray, although a few Blacks attended UW in the late 1800s. Harvey Long, a doctoral student and archivist informed me that William Noland from Binghamton, New York, graduated in 1875 and attended law school for two semesters. Long's (2016) research report states that a few Blacks matriculated on the UW campus up until the 1940s; afterward, especially in the 1960s, their numbers increased. According to Long (2016), "Black students were more integrated into the campus's intellectual life than its social life." Black students were not permitted to join fraternities or sororities.

Off campus, there was a history of overt racism and microaggressions. In 1921, the Ku Klux Klan placed an advertisement in the *Wisconsin State Journal* seeking members for a "fraternal order," and the KKK staged its first parade in Madison. In 1924, wearing conic masks and white robes, the Klan paraded down King Street. In 1958, an African American woman interviewed for a teaching job with the Madison School District but was not hired because the interview committee chair believed that the parents of White students would be against a Black teacher teaching their children (Long, n. d.). Eleven years after the interview of the African American teacher, Gloria, Bob, and I were supervisors to predominately White student teachers in Madison and surrounding schools. As representatives of UW, we were initially warmly accepted into schools. However, as we encouraged the UW student teachers we supervised to correct the racially biased curriculum, to prepare teaching plans that were inclusive, and to stop teaching the one or two African American children in the class from a deficit perspective, we received strong push back from the schools. Phone calls were made to the program director and our advisor, John Antes. He was told to "reign" us in. We had no right to interfere with the Madison school curriculum. That is not what we were doing; we were preparing our teacher candidates to teach all children in Wisconsin. Antes understood what we were trying to do and supported it. However, he would tell us about the phone calls and ask us to be more strategic. "Stirring" by Blacks to eliminate racism is usually met with immediate harsh resistance. Challenges to White self-interest are unacceptable.

Gloria, Bob, and I knew what we were up against. We didn't fear consequences in part because we believed that Antes had our backs. Also, we could return to our positions with CPS, but more importantly, we knew we were on the right side of justice and good teaching. Du Bois (1920) wrote,

> Degrading of men by men is as old as mankind and the invention of no one race or people. . . . It has been left, however, to Europe and to modern days to discover the eternal world-wide mark of meanness,—color!

(p. 24)

In the early 1970s, I began attending the American Education Research Conference (AERA). AERA is the largest organization of education researchers in the United States. AERA brings together between 12,000 and 16,000 researchers, including the best and brightest in the field, at the annual conference. When I first started to attend, I would generously estimate about 25–50 Black researchers, including graduate students like myself, were present or held a membership. Only one or two, or more often no, Black researchers were on the AERA key research committees. These committees conducted research for upcoming and existing policy for the state and federal governments and other entities. From the conference sessions I attended for several years, I observed the research and study of the education of the Black child, the family, and/or community of the Black child was primarily, if not completely, conducted by White researchers. As I listened to the papers and read articles in AERA journals, I was troubled by the biased assumptions, the narrow focus of research questions (e.g., deficit assumptions), and the papers and articles' conclusions and discussions. I then begin to inquire: "How can I get into AERA's inner circle?" Once I received my PhD, I wanted to have a voice in the research on Black students and communities. However, I was stuck in the Veil. DuBois's discussion of the veil/color line and the Veil has become increasingly meaningful as I observe other Black and Brown scholars who have acquired knowledge and skills at premier US universities, but are nevertheless limited because of their skin color to remain in a space (Veil) and not be accepted equally as Whites. It wasn't about me, or my Black and Brown scholar colleagues personally and our academic abilities; it was about our skin color.

I was, for my first 20 years as a member of AERA, trapped, much like Du Bois's character John ("On the Coming of John"; see Chapter 1). I had, like John, received my education—earned my PhD, including taking all the necessary research courses— at a top ranked US university noted for conducting education research. I was now ready to bring my knowledge of research, education literature, and methodology, along with my ideas on schooling in urban spaces, into the closed places where White researchers constructed research questions that made Black students the object of the research in ways that contributed to keeping them behind the veil. However, like John, I learned that the veil/color line (e.g., limitation of opportunity, fear of the Black man and women) that existed within AERA and the attitude of White superiority and privilege among mostly male White researchers was a barrier. I had naively hoped that with the Civil Rights Movement in recent memory, the color line, or *Carl's (black skin) as a problem*, would be changing. Du Bois's character, John, and I both re-learned our lesson; the veil/color line is difficult to tear away, and we were sentenced to live within the Veil and only able to critique the research after it was published.

Two years after I graduated, I was hired as an assistant professor in the C&I Department at UW. One of my responsibilities was to direct the student-teacher program. The same program Gloria, Bob, and I had worked in as supervisors of student teachers when we first arrived. As I got to better know the cooperating teachers whom UW students were assigned to student teach, one told me how the work Gloria, Bob, and I had done with the student teachers to encourage more cultural relevance in the curriculum was received by teachers in the schools. She stated, "Carl, they [Madison teachers] wanted the three of you to leave Madison instantly and go back to Chicago." And when I followed up and asked, "What about you?" She laughed and said, "At the time, I would have escorted your car to the state line."

As our children, Carl and Alicia, moved closer to school age and I earned tenure, it looked like Madison was going to be "home." Gloria and I were faced with the challenge most parents struggle with: where to enroll our kids in school. Carl had attended a Montessori school for three years and Alicia for a few months. We knew from supervising student teachers in the

Madison schools that Black children suffered in the classroom, so we had to be extremely careful in the school we chose. We decided on Shorewood Hills Elementary School, where many of the international graduate students who came to study at UW sent their children, as our best option. Shorewood staff recognized the diversity—mostly international diversity—of students attending the school and responded with international celebration days, books in the school library that told stories of children in other lands, and outreach to the students' parents. A food, fairs, and festival curriculum, although far from being good multicultural education, the faculty and staff, nevertheless, showed some respect for diversity. It was the best we could hope for at the time in Madison. We bought a home in Shorewood and settled in.

Many of Du Bois's ideas and statements continually crisscrossed through my mind during my early years in Madison. I had dealt with race and racism on a professional and personal level, but now I had a family to think about and two young defenseless Black children. I found my space and decided which battles I could and should fight, and how I would accept success and push back on defeat in those racial/microaggression wars. I accepted that if our children and other Black and Brown children at the school were enjoying and learning, Gloria and I were "good." There is so much in my reading of Du Bois that allows me to both to understand my location within the Veil and to be angry about the construction of the high walls of racism that keep me and other Black and Brown people from seeing the sun (full acceptance of Black and Brown humanity in all spaces and places) as I struggled at the color line. There is also much I take away from Du Bois (1920) about White people that remains consistent in their attitude and action, and defines the struggle at the color line today:

> Everything great and good, efficient, fair, and honorable is "white," everything mean, bad, blundering, cheating, and dishonorable is "yellow," a bad taste is "brown," and the devil is "black." The change of this theme is continually rung in picture and story, in newspaper heading and moving-picture and in sermon and school book, until, of course, the King can do no wrong—a White Man is always right and a Black Man has no rights which a White man is bound to respect.
>
> (Du Bois, 1920, p. 8)

After concluding Chapter 2, I move to Chapter 3, where I write about Du Bois's influence on my theorizing and application of multicultural education: "I believe that all men [and women] . . . are brothers [and sisters]" (Du Bois, 1904, p. 1).

References

African American Registry. (2013). Heritage. Available online: www.aaregistry.org/ (accessed 12 June 2016).

Du Bois, W. E. B. (1898). *The Negroes of Farmville, Virginia: A social study, issue 14 of bulletin of bureau of labor*. Washington, DC, US: Government Printing.

Du Bois, W. E. B. (1899). *The Philadelphia Negro*. Philadelphia: University of Pennsylvania Press.

Du Bois, W. E. B. (1903a/1994a). *The souls of black folk*. New York: Dover.

Du Bois, W. E. B. (1903b). The Talented Tenth. Teaching American History.org. Available online: http://teachingamericanhistory.org./library/document/the-talent-tenth/ (accessed 27 March 2016).

Du Bois, W. E. B. (1904). *Credo: Independent*. Memphis, TN: Ed. L. Simon and Company

Du Bois, W. E. B. (1920). Darkwater. NY: Dover. p. 78.

Du Bois, W. E. B. (1925). *Darkwater: Voices from within the veil*. New York: Harcourt, Brace and Howe.

Du Bois, W. E. B. (1926). Criteria of Negro Art. *The Crisis*, October. Available online: http://nationalhumanitiescenter.org/pds/maai3/protest/text10/text10read.htm (accessed 10 May 2016).

Du Bois, W. E. B. (1935). *Black reconstruction*. New York: Harcourt, Brace and Company.

Du Bois, W. E. B. (1940). *Dusk of dawn: An essay toward an autobiography*. New York: Oxford.

Du Bois, W. E. B. (1957/1963). The Last Message to the World, Read at His Funeral in 1963. Compiled by Kathleen E. Bethel, African American Studies Librarian, Northwestern University Library; Adi, Hakim, and Marika Sherwood, American Library Association, 32, 2–6.

Eppse, M. R. (1943). *The Negro, too, in American history*. Nashville: National publication Co.

Frazier, F. E. (1939). *Negro family in the United States*. Chicago: University of Chicago Press.

Greenlee, S. (1969). *The spook who sat by the door: A novel*. London: Allison & Busby.

King, M. L. KL. Jr. (n. d.). "I Fear I May Have Integrated My People Into a Burning House." https://ourcommonground.com/2013/08/20/i-fear-i-may-have-integrated-my-people-into-a-burning-house-martin-luther-king-jr/. accessed 4/2/17.

Long, H. (2016). *African-Americans at the University of Wisconsin (1875–1969)*. Madison, WI: UW-Madison News.

Long, H. D. (n.d.). African-Americans at the University of Wisconsin (1875–1969). UW Archives. Available online: www.library.wisc.edu/archives/exhibits/campus-history-projects/african-americans-at-the-university-of-wisconsin-1875-1969/ (accessed 2 August 2016).

McIntosh, P. (1989). *White privilege: Unpacking the invisible knapsack*. S.I.

United States (1965). *The Negro family: The case for national action*. Washington: For sale by the Supt. of Docs., U.S. Govt. Print. Off.

Viadero, D. (2006). Race Report's Influence Felt 40 Years Later. *EdWeek*. Available online: Edweek-2006-on-the-Coleman-Report-and-its-legacy (accessed 9 May 2016).

Woodson, C. G. (1933). *The mis-education of the Negro*. Chicago: African American Images.

3

MULTICULTURALISTS IN THE SUNSHINE OF DU BOIS

In this chapter, I discuss Du Bois's influence—his sunshine—on my theorizing about each of the marginalized groups under the multicultural umbrella. Du Bois recognized diversity in his scholarship and argued that a humane society should strive for fellowship and should address social problems because of the intrinsic value of all humanity. I borrow from Du Bois's construction of "problem" to frame my discussion of each marginalized group under the multicultural umbrella: race, gender, people living on or below the poverty line, gay and lesbian people, transgendered people, and people who have a disability are viewed as a *problem.* These groups don't enjoy the blessings of liberty stipulated in the US Constitution, and globally they live behind the veil/color line.

Conceptualization of Multicultural Education

I see the 1970s as the period that enabled the rise of multicultural education (MCE) and a heightening of the awareness of multiculturalism in the United States. In doing so, I acknowledge that earlier Black, Brown, Red, Yellow, and White scholars gave attention to multicultural America and a world that inhabited culturally diverse communities. In the early 1970s, I, along with a small group of multiracial and gender-inclusive young scholars, saw the United States and the world in ways that many others were not seeing it and didn't want to imagine it. We accepted and promoted the humanity of all humans and wanted to develop education policy(ies) and implement education practice(s) that promotes education equality and equity for all students. In doing so, we knew that systemic racism in most, if not all, societal institutions and structures would resist our efforts because they were not fostering the inclusion of marginalized group members as part of their membership or mission and purpose. In addition, we knew that Whites who promoted domination and oppression of people of color in one of its many forms—privilege, exploitation, and denial of opportunity—didn't want change and would go to great lengths, almost any length, to resist change.

Today, this problem is better, but far from adhering to the expectations and promises of a democracy. As members of the multiracial and gender-inclusive group developed their area(s) of educational research and scholarship, we concluded that "multicultural education," more so than ethnic studies and other models of education addressing student diversity, was a more appropriate and meaningful conceptualization. "Multicultural education," we argued, was the appropriate term to use to address and prize America's diversity. Multicultural education, we contended, should be directed at the policy and practice inequities in America education associated with race, socioeconomic class, disability, sexual orientation, and gender. In addition, Multiculturalists contended that the ideology guiding American education needs to advocate for all students to acquire the knowledge, skills, and dispositions to flourish in a racially, ethnically, socioeconomically, and culturally diverse nation and world. Multiculturalists argued that multicultural education, as an ideology and practice, with attention directed toward the flourishing of the humanity of each student, should permeate all aspects of school practices, policies, and organizations to ensure the highest levels of academic and social achievement for all students. A multicultural curriculum, multiculturalists posit, includes the histories, cultures, and contributions of all American cultural groups and should directly address issues of racism, sexism, classism, linguicism, ableism, ageism, and heterosexism, as well as religious intolerance and xenophobia. Multiculturalists believed, in keeping with America's democratic project, all students should be taught to work actively toward structural equality and to tear away the veil/color line in society's organizations and institutions. When we as multiculturalists announced these goals, we knew we were in for a long struggle and that our generation would probably not see them come to fruition, but it was important to us to lay a solid foundation for the struggle and to proceed with it for as long as possible.

My understanding of the inclusiveness of multicultural education was further informed when I came across Du Bois's (1952) essay "Negro and the Warsaw Ghetto," in *Jewish Life*. As I read Du Bois's essay, I saw how a researcher's "question/problem" evolves, expands, and shines a bright light on his work. Du Bois explained that his travel to German Poland introduced him to a new race problem after World War II: "There, I realized another problem of race or religion, I don't know which, which had to do with the treatment and segregation of large numbers of human beings" (p. 45). Du Bois's continues, "I became aware of the Jewish problem of the modern world and something of its history. . . . It never occurred to me until then that any exhibition of race prejudice could be anything but color prejudice" (p. 46). Du Bois's discovery of another problem of injustice and another group of people oppressed because of something other than a color line was like advocates of multicultural education discovering that attention must be given to people with disabilities and understanding their physical or mental challenge was compounded by race, class, sexual orientation, and other positionalities.

Du Bois (1952) writes,

> [M]y view of the Warsaw ghetto, was not so much a clearer understanding of the Jewish problem in the world as it was a real and complete understanding of the Negro problem . . . the problem of slavery, emancipation and caste in the United States was no longer in my mind a separate and unique thing as I had long conceived it. It was not even solely a matter of color and physical and racial characteristics, which was particularly a hard thing for me to learn, since for a lifetime the color line had been a real and efficient cause of misery.
>
> (p. 45)

Here Du Bois reminds multiculturalists that the many forms of oppression are linked (intersect) and that they all contribute to dehumanization. As Du Bois (1952) moves toward the conclusion of the essay, he warns of the breadth and depth of racial oppression and the extent to which it is structurally situated. His last line reads,

No, the race problem in which I was interested, cut across lines of color and physique and belief and status and was a matter of cultural patterns, perverted teaching and human hate and prejudice which reach all sorts of people and cause endless evil to all men.

(p. 46)

Du Bois's (1952) final sentence in the essay spoke to multiculturalists in several ways: Du Bois was informing multiculturalists that racism brings oppression, exploitation, and reduced opportunity: people of color's social class status is reduced, women of color are considered second to White women, and people of color who have a disability are viewed as less valuable.

Du Bois was an advocate for *any people* who were denied justice, and Du Bois wanted his observation to point out that understanding a *problem* demands continual attention and a willingness to have your understanding evolve. Du Bois argued that the ghetto of Warsaw "helped me to emerge from a certain social provincialism into a broader conception of what the fight against race segregation, religious discrimination, and oppression by wealth had to become if civilization was going to triumph and broaden the world" (p. 46). Du Bois's identification of, description of, and response to the color line and its intersection with socioeconomic class and gender were central to the formation of my ideas on multicultural education. That said, Du Bois did not outwardly promote gender, and I haven't discovered his perspective on disability, gays, and lesbians. Whereas he explored the link between race and social class, his theorizing of the problem for marginalized groups did not include, or was reluctant to include, gender. Why this was so, arguably, is puzzling, especially because several of his Black female colleagues, such as Anna Julia Cooper, had a growing body of literature that addressed the intersection of race, gender, and class. Du Bois would have had to know about Cooper's scholarship and her work at M Street School in Washington, DC. Her book *A Voice from the South by a Woman from the South* was published in 1892, 11 years before *Souls*. In addition, she spoke at the first Pan-African Conference along with Du Bois. Her speech "The Negro Problem in America," according to the archival record, seems to be lost. That said, Cooper's focus was on women. One of Cooper's (1892) more noted statements is "not the boys less, the girls more," which captures the thrust and tenor of her work. In addition, Coleman (2017) argues, "Du Bois couldn't have had that last important phase of this life with the partnership of had with Shirley" Graham DuBois, his second wife (p. 1). Graham was a very accomplished person in her own right, authoring *Tom-Tom*, the first all-Black opera performed professionally in the United States (Coleman, 2017).

The early advocates came to the discussion of multicultural education with an understanding that there were numerous marginalized groups that must be collectively and equally included under the multiculturalist umbrella. Next, I discuss marginalized groups under the multicultural umbrella, and although I discuss them separately to give historical context, several of the advocates, including myself, saw them as a collective entity.

Constituents Under the Multicultural Umbrella

Race as a Problem: Founding Constituent of MCE

During the conceptualization of multicultural education, there were debates over which marginalized groups should be included. Race, or people of color, was a founding constituent of the multicultural education movement because people of color as a *problem* is the object of systemic oppression that needed total change. In 1947, Du Bois, tired and worn from more than 50 years of struggle to have Black people treated as full citizens in America, went to the United Nations General Assembly to appeal to the world about the *problem*. Du Bois's argument contributed to the groundwork for multiculturalists' rationale for placing race under the multicultural umbrella. Du Bois's (1947) speech, "An Appeal to the World: A Statement of Denial of Human Rights to Minorities," stated that Blacks were a segregated caste, stolen from Africa and enslaved, denied the right to vote, mis-educated, forced into poverty, and referenced as "other persons" (three-fifths) in the US Constitution. Du Bois presented data on lynching, segregation, Jim Crow, and inequalities in education, housing, health care, and the voting rights of Black people. The data chronicled the horror of the treatment of Blacks in America. Du Bois concluded his address to the United Nations General Assembly with the following: "No nation is so great that the world can afford to let it continue to be deliberately unjust, cruel and unfair toward its own citizens" (p. 3). Du Bois's speech was one that all people of color could connect with, because Hispanic Americans, Native Americans, and Asian Americans all knew they are seen as less than by Whites.

The Civil Rights Movement was also in the thoughts of multiculturalists as they placed marginalized groups under the multicultural umbrella. Race was central in the Civil Rights Movement, which had only recently ended. The multiculturalists, whom I was meeting with, were pleased with some of the gains made in the 1960s, but remained frustrated with civil rights gains made in education, housing, and employment.

Schools remained segregated. Multiculturalists argued that it was past time for the humanity of children of color to be fully accepted and respected; no longer should students of color have to put up with White supremacy and be passive in the face of White privilege. Parents of English language learners wanted their culture and language included in their children's education. Native American parents demanded correction to their portrayal as "the noble savage" and being located mainly in historical times in textbooks. Also, they demanded that all students learn about American Indian sovereignty and to respect natural resources. Black parents demanded the elimination of the deficit ideologies and practices, low academic expectations, and negative stereotypical thinking about their children. In addition, Black parents argued that their history, culture, and gifts to the United States should be included in the school curriculum. Asian Americans questioned being referenced to as "model minorities." Also, they argued that Asian Americans are Americans, and many people, upon meeting them, should not assume they are "foreigners." The problem of the structural racism that parents of color identified as hurting their children, multiculturalists knew, would entail a long struggle.

Du Bois's work was informative because it pushed me to think about "race" in more complex, complicated, and nuanced frames. I more clearly understood "the problem of the color line, not simply as a national and personal question but rather in its larger world aspect in time and space" (Du Bois, 1900, p. 1). I considered race and racism as it affected all people in the United States (people of color and White people). In addition, Du Bois's work contributed to the way I considered race and racism on a global level: how groups of color live within a majority society, how children born of marriage between a mother who is an immigrant and a father who is a citizen of a country are treated in society, and how immigration and migration was increasing worldwide.

As a young scholar, I found Du Bois's notion of being a *problem* significant in my research and the challenges I faced as a multicultural scholar working at a predominately White research university. Early on in my tenure, I saw that the institutionalizing of things that were not White was a *problem*, and the *problem* was always managed to satisfy White concerns as much as possible. The establishment of Asian, Black, Latino, and Native American studies departments and programs on the UW campus was a *problem*—a *problem* that could have fractured relationships between groups of color, because only Blacks were permitted to have a department and other ethnic groups were given program status. However, members within the groups of color "would not bleach [their] his Negro soul in a flood of white Americanism" (Du Bois, 1903, p. 2). Du Bois's argument that the color line was about the relationship between races—White versus Black, White versus Brown, White versus Red, White versus Yellow, and White versus the total collective of people of color. The relationship, Du Bois argued, was essentially one of domination, exploitation, or self-interest. Also, as a young scholar, reading Du Bois not only reminded me that positive racial change comes with a struggle, but also that there is politics within change. In addition, I learned that despite thoroughness and dedication, and accuracy of data produced to bring about change, racial change is difficult to come by. Du Bois learned this lesson and reported it in *The Philadelphia Negro* in 1899. *Philadelphia* was a first of its kind: an in-depth, well-conceptualized, and meticulously conducted sociological study of the social and economic conditions of Blacks living in the 7th Ward of

Philadelphia. Du Bois hoped that the research data reported would convince Whites that their knowledge of Blacks was based on flawed race theory and evolutionary science and a mis-reading of biblical scriptures. In addition, Du Bois (1899) argued,

> White people of the city must remember that much of the sorrow and bitterness that surrounds the life of the American Negro comes from the unconscious prejudice and half-conscious actions of men and women who do not intend to wound or annoy.

(pp. 396–397)

Du Bois, however, would soon come to learn that Whites' prejudice and racism are not unconsciousness or half-conscious actions, but many are planned and organized efforts to oppress the marginalized groups, who are included under the multicultural umbrella.

Philadelphia was ignored by Whites and structural racism continued as if the study had never taken place. Although Du Bois considered his monumental effort a failure, it neverthe-less provided me and other people of color a reality check about Whites and the racial struggle. We learned that the struggle would be intense, and more than sociological and his-torical data were needed to change Whites' racist attitudes and actions toward Blacks. Du Bois's sociological and historical research data and arguments about the flawed theorizing of Black inferiority was not accepted by Whites. Also, Du Bois's plea to Philadelphia's Black and White communities to work together in trying to resolve "the Negro problems,"—that is, racial prejudice and discrimination, and denying or making it difficult for Blacks to get decent jobs and keep them—was disregarded.

Low Socioeconomic Status as a Problem: *Founding Constituent of MCE*

Socioeconomic status (SES) was another founding constituent of multicultural education. The knowledge of variation in wealth, power, privilege, material possession, authority, and prestige among people in US society is well known and established. These variations produce different social classes or "classes" of people. Sociologists refer to the variations as the horizontal stratification of populations into upper class, upper middle, lower middle, working class, and poor (Gordon, 1949). Being of low social class (working class, poor) or SES, multiculturalists argue, leads to fewer opportunities in terms of health care, leisure, employment, and education. The lack of wealth and education, multiculturalists contended, leads upper-class and upper-middle-class people to falsely believe that people who are working class and poor are not equal to them. However, multiculturalists argue that the construction of working class and poor people as inferior is flawed. Growing up in Bronzeville, and observing working class, poor, middle, and upper-middle-class people, I knew better. In addition, what I observed in Bronzeville was corroborated by scholars such as Du Bois, and others pushed back on the fallacious narrative that wealth makes one person better than the next. Connecting money, wealth, and education to arguments that rich people are more equal than poor people has a long history as part of the White supremacy thesis that acts against low-income Blacks and Whites to keep both in the low-income status group. The Blacks are inferior trope and racism made poor White workers gullible to the White supremacy thesis that influenced their social class and the social class of people of color. Du Bois (1935b) argued because Whites have been erroneously misconceived that Black and other people of color are not equal to Whites, it prevents them from seeing "The Gifts of Black Folk." In addition, the Whites are superior thesis prevented low-income "White workers from seeing low income Black workers as workers" (Bracey, n. d., p. 2). Instead, White low-income workers see Black workers and other workers of color as inferior and takers of their jobs. Whites' racism enabled both low-income Whites and low-income Blacks to be financially taken advantage of, as wealthy White employers bargain over salaries, causing Whites to compete against Blacks.

Black Reconstruction illuminated how climbing up the SES ladder is racially governed and how SES intersects with race. Du Bois (1935a) wrote,

> Here is the real modern labor problem. . . . The emancipation of man is the emancipation of labor, and the emancipation of labor is the freeing of that basic majority of workers who are yellow, brown and black.

(p. 6)

Green and Smith (1983) do correctly note that although Du Bois's attention to class is not considered equal to his attention to race, his work did give a great deal of attention to the class struggle. Green and Smith (1983) argue that in a paper titled "A Constructive Critique of Wage Theory: An Essay on the Present State of Economic Theory in Regard to Wages," Du Bois pointed out to leading European scholars of political economy that their work didn't include a systematic theory of wages. In the essay, Du Bois (1891) raised a question that is relevant to workers today: "What is the cause of difference in higher classes of labor?" Answering his queries as he often did, Du

Bois's (1891) response has currency with workers today who are refused a decent ($15.00 per hour) minimum wage. Du Bois (1891) stated, "Wages are determined by the wants of the capitalists" (Du Bois, quoted in Green and Smith, 1983, p. 205).

In *The Philadelphia Negro* (1899), Du Bois pointed out race and class distinctions and argued how the exclusion of Blacks from good jobs, homes/housing in financially stable neighborhoods, and structural racism kept Blacks as working class or poor. In *Philadelphia* (1899), Du Bois's interview scale asked, "What sub-group and classes exist?" As Green and Smith (1983) argue, Du Bois's class and race analysis in *Philadelphia* (1899) enabled him to perceptively comprehend and point out the social reality of Blacks in Philadelphia.

Throughout his work, Du Bois focused on the "material force of racism" and examined the structures that make up SES such as education, income, and occupation. Writing in *The Crisis*, "The Class Struggle," Du Bois (1921) offered Black Americans a statement that many Black and Brown workers would support today:

> Theoretically we are part of the world proletariat in the sense that we are mainly an exploited class of cheap laborers; but, practically we are not a part of the white proletariat to any great extent. We are the victims of their physical oppression, social ostracism, economic exclusion and personal hatred.
>
> (*The Crisis*, 22 August, 151)

In addition, Du Bois argued that "class struggle" refers to "the natural antagonism and war between the exploiter and the exploited." In 2011, Wisconsin workers witnessed Du Bois's observation in real time as their collective bargaining power was taken away despite days of protest at the state capitol.

Act 10, legislation proposed by the governor and passed by the Wisconsin legislature, rolled back collective bargaining powers of public workers. Since the legislation was passed, there has been nearly a 40% reduction in union membership in the state that is the birthplace of the public-employee union. Wisconsin public schoolteachers in numerous districts who were already using their own personal funds to supplement needed class-room supplies saw their base salaries and fringe benefits drop an average of $2,095 to $5,580 (Johnson, 2016).

During the final weeks of completing *Du Bois and Education*—late 2016 to early 2017—my break from writing was reading the popular press on days I wasn't teaching. Increasingly, I noticed a swell of articles and heard commentary that the newly elected president's policies would hurt the low- and middle-income White voters (rural, rust belt, coal country) who put him in office. As I continued to follow "why the white working class votes against itself" discourse (see, for example, Rampell, 2016), I noticed that the statements by those interviewed for the articles were classist and racist.

> That son of a b—is making $10 an hour! I'm making $13.13. I feel like s—because he's making almost as much as I am, and I have never been in trouble with the law and I have a clean record, I can pass a drug test.
>
> (Rampell, 2016)

> A recent *YouGov/Huffington Post survey* found that Trump voters are five times more likely to believe that "average Americans" have gotten less than they deserve in recent years than to believe that "blacks" have gotten less than they deserve. [African Americans don't count as "average Americans," apparently.]
>
> (Rampell, 2016)

Du Bois's observation in a 1937 article "The Nucleus of Class Consciousness" has a great deal of relevance for white working-class voters, "so long as American labor is more conscious of color and race than it is of the fundamental economic needs of the whole laboring class; just so long, the development of labor solidarity is impossible" (p. 23)

Black Reconstruction in America 1860–1880 (Du Bois, 1935a) was my reading during the summer months of 1970. The 700-page tome was an education about the history of Black people's role in reconstructing an interracial democracy, enslavement as the vehicle of America's rise to prominence as an industrial nation, and the Black experience as part of the American labor movement. Reading *Black Reconstruction* was informative and enjoyable, because I enjoy Du Bois the most when he is getting after someone or something. *Black Reconstruction*, I would contend, was first and foremost written to correct the inaccuracies and lies told by eminent White historians about Blacks, such as their inability to govern during Reconstruction and their inferiority as a race, to feed a systemic narrative to keep Blacks poor, lacking in education, and working menial jobs. *Black Reconstruction* also told of class struggle, of labor's exploitation, the difficulty Blacks had controlling their own labor, ownership of labor, and how unemployed Black men could be deemed "vagrants," seized, and auctioned off as laborers in order to pay fines. Du Bois (1935a) additionally told of freedmen who were required to turn over the property they had been working as their own. They were commanded to give up the land and forgo their dream of economic independence and land ownership because emancipated enslaved people had no money to purchase land.

Du Bois (1935a) was pointing out how Blacks were succeeding in their struggle against the color line despite Whites' efforts to incur Black failure that would then cause Blacks to see themselves in negative ways and not be able to see their truer self. Du Bois pointed out to Whites and wanted Blacks to know that, although Blacks falsely were considered a *problem*, they had the ability to govern and, more importantly, to take care of home and family.

During my early years on the tenure track at UW, many of the graduate students were reading Samuel Bowles and Herbert Gintis (1976). Bowls and Gintis promoted the "correspondence theory," which argued that schools serve a purpose in society and prepared students for jobs in keeping with the hierarchical relations of work and production that are mirrored in the relations we see in schools. Bowles and Gintis's (1976) thesis contended that the economic status of the students' families, rather than school or educational achievement, is the best predictor of students' future economic status. Bowles and Gintis's (1976) ideas were the arguments offered by many graduates for the lack of success of Black students and other students of color. Whereas I found Bowles and Gintis's (1976) ideas meaningful, I was concerned because the intersection of class and race were undertheorized and little attention was given to the variation among people, their social class notwithstanding. Bowles and Gintis's (1976) argument was deterministic. People' agency and the opportunities people received were understated. I welcomed analyses that illuminated the "problem" in urban areas, but not at the expense of underplaying historical problems as Du Bois emphasized in *Philadelphia* and *Black Reconstruction*, and/or that understated the significance of an intersectional analysis of class, race, and gender, and/or assigned Blacks to a position in society void of historical progress and aspiration. I knew from growing up in Bronzeville and hearing firsthand about the Great Migration of Blacks from the South to get jobs and have better social, political, and economic opportunities; from reading about Mexicans' immigration and diffusion into and throughout the United States from the 1840s onward in order to live better economically and socially; and from learning about Chinese immigrants' journeys to the United States to work in gold mines and on the Transcontinental Railroad in order to send money back to China to support their families that for people of color, upward mobility in society is not governed by a deterministic thesis.

Drawing on Du Bois, I argued when I was being bombarded with arguments from Bowls and Gintis in my classes that offered a multicultural perspective that social structures can be changed and that they remain the way they were because of racism. I argued that "race" is socially constructed and although it is interpreted and given meaning in public and private spaces, geographically, individuals are not locked in; they have agency, despite the color line. I contended that poor people have agency and pointed out the slow, but steady, increases of both Black and White students on campus who were first-generation college students. I asked, "How many of you are first-generation college students?" "Why did it take you so long to get here with all of your White privileges?" "Consider the challenges of people of color, who were only "equally" accepted on the UW campus less than ten years ago, in comparison with your challenges."

Gender as a Problem: Founding Constituent of MCE

The inclusion of gender under the multicultural umbrella caused some debate. Some multiculturalists argued that the feminist movement was underway, and White women would consider the inclusion of gender as invading their turf; additionally, White women leading the feminist movement ignored women of color, because they believed that women of color were less than they were. Women of color, however, contended that gender, with or without White middle-class women, should be included, especially since many poor White women were also oppressed by patriarchy. Women of color, multiculturalists argued, were positioned within structures of power differently than White women; they were doubly oppressed (e.g., racism and gender) and many were triply oppressed (sexism, racism, and classism), and therefore deserved to be included under the multicultural umbrella. Sojourner Truth's (1851) "Ain't I a Woman" speech became my point of reference during discussions. Truth, an emancipated enslaved person, delivered a speech that spoke to the humanity of Black women as "women" in totality. In her speech delivered at the (White) Women's Convention in Akron, Ohio, Truth said, "That man over there says that women need to be helped into carriages and lifted over ditches ... Nobody ever helps me into carriages, or over mud-puddles ... ain't I a woman?" (p. 2).

Gender, under the multicultural umbrella, advocates against patriarchy, empowers women and girls, and demands that women and men have the same rights and opportunities within all systems in society. In addition, multiculturalists argued that women's history and stories should be equally centered as the history and stories of men. Multiculturalists railed against the construction of gender subordination and gender as a *problem*. But, as Du Bois noted, *all* is a problem that are not White, male, or owners of capital.

When I looked back at the arguments I made during the debate for the inclusion of gender under the multicultural umbrella, Du Bois's idea of a *problem* was significant, but my ideas were more influenced by my reading of Anna Julie Cooper (1892)—noted earlier—than by the work of Du Bois. Cooper was an educator, author, activist, intellectual, and womanist (Grant, Brown, and Brown, 2016), and she was among the first Black intellectuals (1897) to initiate theorizing about the intersections of race, gender, and class, and their significance in policy, economics, education, and social science in general, including research and daily life (Washington, 1988). Du Bois was acknowledged as an advocate for women's suffrage, as noted in his 1915 *Crisis* article where he stated, "This month 200,000 Negro voters will be called upon to vote on the question of giving the right of suffrage to women. THE CRISIS sincerely trusts that every one of them will vote Yes" (1915b, p. 29–30). Nevertheless, Du Bois has been heavily criticized about his treatment of women as professional equals. In his article from 1898 titled "The Study of the Negro Problem," he posited a model of a scholar who analyzed the Negro problem as male. In other writings, the most exemplary "The Damnation of Women," Du Bois (1920) focuses his attention on Black women as mothers, workers, and activists, but not as intellectuals (p. 28). Du Bois's identification of a *problem* pervades my work on gender and multicultural education policy and practice. But Du Bois's lack of inclusiveness of outstanding female colleagues of his generation called for caution in including his scholarship to directly support gender issues. Griffin (2000) states, "Du Bois was sexist, just as he was elitist and 'color struck.'" Guy-Sheftall (1990) argues that Du Bois "idealized the image of black women, much in the same way that southern white men paid homage to the shrine of [White] womanhood" (p. 161), by inferring that women are the weaker sex and must be protected by their men from the world. James (1997) contends that Du Bois believed that men were more intelligent than women and that as he argued for women's rights,

"He veiled the individual achievements of women . . . from the political landscape" (p. 37). Multiculturalists and *Du Bois and Education* are reminded that because of Du Bois's sexist behavior or narrow inclusion of female colleagues (and I believe the former, more so than the latter), his personal beliefs must be vetted, and the acceptance of the humanity of each person or group of people should not be undercut in any way.

Sexual Orientation as a Problem: *A Contested Constituent of MCE*

Du Bois (1903/1994, 1920, 1952) was a firm believer that inequality grounded in structures could be changed and that change and reform should be fought for. My belief in Du Bois's logic, that inequality grounded in structure could be changed, was put to a test in the 1980s as I participated in arguments to include sexual orientation under the multicultural umbrella. Multiculturalists were struggling in every arena of education to hold firm to the gains of the 1960s, as they continued their efforts to establish race and gender equality, and to have low-income people not ostracized because of the conditions in which they were living. As I thought about the fight over sexual orientation, I knew it would be a challenge, because some multiculturalists were against placing it under the multicultural umbrella. Sexual orientation was a *problem* that many educators didn't wanted to discuss. Sexual orientation was not in the schools' official curriculum, and textbook publishers did not include it. A student who was searching for answers about sexual orientation would not be able to find a book in the school. Teacher preparation programs, as well as administrative license programs, didn't include discussions of gay and lesbian students. Race, gender, and social class as problems were publicly debated. Sexual orientation was negatively whispered about. The numerous sessions at education conferences that dealt with the inclusion of sexual orientation under the multicultural umbrella were full of robust debate. Opposition was grounded in Christianity, moral discourses, and discourses of fear. Some argued, for example, that "a gay teacher will influence their daughter or son to become gay."

In 1926, Du Bois was a part of a small group, somewhat like the multiculturalist group I was involved with, that was pushing for structural change in the way White people viewed Negro art. The group of multiculturalists that I was working with to include sexual orientation under the multicultural umbrella, I thought, would benefit from Du Bois's (1926) words:

> I do not doubt but there are some in this audience who are a little disturbed at the subject of this meeting, and particularly at the subject I have chosen. Such people are thinking something like this: "How is it that an organization like this, a group of radicals trying to bring new things into the world, a fighting organization which has come up out of the blood and dust of battle, struggling for the right of black men to be ordinary human beings—how is it that an organization of this kind can turn aside to talk about Art? After all, what have we who are slaves and black to do with Art?"

> (p. 290)

After about three years of steadfast insistence by several multicultural advocates, sexual orientation became an equal member of the multicultural family. At the National Association for Multicultural Education (NAME) conference in Washington, DC, in 1995, I recall the organization's first openly gay speaker delivering a keynote address. I wondered at the time, as president of NAME, how the membership would respond to the speaker. We thoughtfully scheduled the speech on the second day of the conference at 11 a.m. so everyone would be up and breakfast would be over, and a highly regarded NAME member did the introduction. The ballroom where the speech was given was packed, and after the address, the audience rose and delivered a standing ovation that lasted more than two minutes. Recalling the event reminds me of the good days on this journey to recognize and respect all humanity, and it argues that people's ways of thinking can change. People can change their views and accept or at least go along with new ways of thinking. Du Bois, in his 1906 "Address to Country," offered words that I often recall when engaged in a tough struggle:

> Courage brothers! The battle for humanity is not lost or losing. All across the skies sit signs of promise. The Slav is raising in his might, the yellow millions are tasting liberty, the black Africans are writhing toward the light, and everywhere the laborer, with ballot in his hand, is voting open the gates of Opportunity and Peace. The morning breaks over blood-stained hills. We must not falter, we may not shrink. Above are the everlasting stars.

Du Bois, based upon my reading, didn't address sexual orientation in his writing. The one connection I discovered was when his daughter, Yolande married renown poet Countee Cullen, who was gay, thus causing his daughter (and Du Bois) a great deal of unrest and a failed marriage.

Disability: As a Problem: A Welcomed Constituent of MCE

Since the early 1800s, when doctor Jean-Marc-Gaspard Itard, taught the "wild boy," Victor of Aveyron, France, a feral child, 11 or 12, basic civil skills and Anne Sullivan Macy developed reading and communication skills between herself and Helen Keller, a child who was deaf and could not speak and blind, society has publicly recognized that some with full membership in humanity need help. That said, school-age children with disabilities such as mental retardation, autism, schizophrenia, and behavioral disorders were, until arguably the 1960s, a *problem* that society largely ignored and did not celebrate their humanity. The Education of all Handicapped Children Act also known as Public Law 94–142 (PL 94 142) was passed in 1975, and the Americans with Disabilities Act (ADA) was passed in 1990. PL 94–142 and the ADA were the federal government's efforts to resolve the *problem*. PL 94–142 stated that the federal government will

> protect the rights of, meeting the individual needs of, and improving the results for infants, toddlers, children, and youths, with disabilities and their families and required schools to provide free, appropriate public education to students with physical and mental disabilities, and emotional and behavioral disorders.
>
> (p. 4)

Schools, per PL 94–142, had to provide the most "least restrictive environment" as possible for students with disabilities to learn. "ADA is a civil rights law that prohibits discrimination against individuals with disabilities in all area of public life, including school, transportation, and public and private places that are open to the general public" (ADA National Network, 1990). PL 94–142 and ADA came to the aid of White children with disabilities, but only some children of color.

Students of color are overrepresented in special education. Currently, Black students make up only 16% of the student population, but occupy as many as 32% of the seats in some special education programs, and this data is similar for Latino students as well (Zorigian and Job, 2015). From a Du Boisian perspective, the overrepresentation of students of color in special education is because of two of the three aspects of the veil/color line: One, their skin color is not white, which leads to them being treated differently in schools: they are a *problem*. Two, Whites do not see students of color as "normal" students. Three, deficit ideology leads teachers to view Black students and Brown students as in need of special treatment.

Multiculturalists readily agreed that "disability" should be included under the multicultural umbrella. All multiculturalists, either as teachers working in a school and/or as researchers reviewing the literature on special education, took issue with the overrepresentation of students of color in special education. Multiculturalists argued that PL 94–142 and ADA were good pieces of legislation, but students of color did not equally benefit from the legislation. Du Bois, from what I could find, did not reference disability in his scholarship. Nevertheless, a Du Boisian notion of the veil/color line is useful in discussing the overrepresentation of students of color in special education, for they live behind a veil and are often challenged by the intersection of several *problems*: race, class, and lack of academic achievement.

Globalization: As a **Problem:** *Old Constituent of MCE With a New Portfolio*

On July 25, 1900, at the closing event of the first Pan-African Conference, Du Bois started on an ambitious journey to free Africa of White supremacy and the brutality that comes with White colonialism and power. Du Bois's speech, a letter titled "Address to the Nations of the World," first called attention to how in the modern world Brown, Asian, White, and Black people were becoming increasing bound together. Du Bois appealed to the leaders of European nations to do away with racism and grant self-governing status to colonies in Africa and the West Indies. The letter was a major step forward in the participation of people of color in global affairs. The letter, written on behalf of the men and women of African blood, addressed the future of the darker races. Du Bois spoke of the need for opportunity, education, and self-development for people of color, and asked how long skin color and hair texture would hold back the progress of civilization.

Du Bois was pointing out how colonialism and imperialism were continuing to expand unfettered across the world. Du Bois argued that prejudice, greed, and injustice were causing the Black world to be exploited, ravished, and degraded. He ended with a plea to the "Great Nations," calling on their humanity, sense of justice, and recognition of righteousness. Although Du Bois's letter was ignored, it called attention to a world that was changing to become "flat" (Friedman, 2005) and the work that needed to be done to free Africa and to liberate people of color all over the world. At "The Races in Conference" in 1910, Du Bois argued for a "real democracy of races and nation" (p. 407, f).

Multiculturalists have been aware, thanks in part to the work of Du Bois, about globalization and both its negative and positive impacts on developing nations. Du Bois's explanation of how Europeans colonized land where people of color live, taking minerals, animals, and other natural resources and changing the culture has been useful to multiculturalists studying globalization. In addition, multiculturalists continue to see people with a darker skin manufactured as a *problem*, and Europeans have little to say about their contribution to the *problem*. Multiculturalists stand on the shoulders of Du

Bois and others to study and analyze current problems of globalization. Multiculturalists contend that the color line and economics controlled by Europeans continue to negatively affect countries governed by people of color and continue to affect people of color wherever they live in large numbers, much like Du Bois described decades ago. As multiculturalists look across the globe, they continue to see race or ethnicity used as a mode of domination, flaring up as an "ideology of justification" for punitive action and used to put in place institutional arrangements (Karenga, 2003/2010).

As I travel and read the work of my graduate students who are conducting research in other countries and host scholars who come to study with me from different countries across the world, my awareness of how globalization and a Eurocentric world perspective is shaping views, values, and economic practices of the "darker people" of the world as it keeps them behind the veil/color line has increased. In "The African Roots of War" Du Bois (1915a) was concerned with how European nations were exploiting African countries. Du Bois again reached out through letters, and other means, to explain to Europe and America that they were not involving people of color in global discussions. Again, Du Bois was ignored. In response to being ignored, Du Bois (1915a) wrote,

> Must the rest of the world be left naked to the inevitable horror of war, especially when we know that it is directly in this outer circle of races, and not in the inner European household, that the real causes of present European fighting are to be found?

> (p. 1)

Du Bois's attention to racial domination and racial and economic exploitation by Europe and America toward countries where mostly darker people live is a scholarly task that multiculturalists continue with today. Similarly, as Du Bois called attention to racial and economic exploitation at the national and international levels, he also spoke of his hope, peace based on justice, mutual respect, and freedom (Du Bois, 1920).

My work and the work of other multiculturalists are also hopeful about globalization. We see the bright side of globalization: health care, education, technology, and, for me personally, professionally engaging through Skype, travel, and coauthoring publications, as well as learning from people of different cultural and religious backgrounds, and having the opportunities to read and hear of their histories. Such work, in a Du Boisian sense, is an attempt to pull back the veil so that people of darker races of the world get to know one another and for White people to see the humanity in all people. This month a graduate student from Barcelona, Spain, who is Roma, and had come to work with me, and I had our last coffee, cake, and discussion together before he returned home. We both listened carefully to one another for one more pleasant time. I then took his insightful comments into my course on Black intellectual thought that afternoon. I reminded the classes that in 2016, the humanity of the darker sisters and brothers, wherever they live and whoever they are, continues to be challenged by racist ideology that is imbedded in history and structured in institutional arrangements. In *Souls* (1903), Du Bois wrote,

> Herein lies the tragedy of the age: not that men are poor,—all men know something of poverty; not that men are wicked,—who is good? not that men are ignorant,—what is Truth? Nay, but men know so little of men.

(pp. 139–140)

Intersectionality: As a **Problem:** *A Welcomed Constituent of MCE*

Intersectionality—the interconnectedness of race, class, gender, sexual orientation, disability, and other marginalized groups—is a concept that multiculturalists argue needed to be understood and considered in education policy and practices. Du Bois's connection of race, social class and national interest, race and imperialism, and race and materialism clarified the complexities of race and wealth. Sojourner Truth made multiculturalists aware of intersectionality during her speech in Akron, Ohio, in 1851 at the Women's Convention, and Anna Julie Cooper conceptually crystallized intersectionality for us regarding women of color. Cooper (1892) argued that women of color are triply oppressed by their race, class, and gender as they navigate social and political life.

Throughout his scholarship, Du Bois argued that the color line demands a multidimensional analysis to identify and understand the intersections of race and class as both modes of domination and modes of resistance on the national and global levels (Sdonline, 2011). In his essays and lectures on race and inequality, Du Bois made a connection between race and economic inequality, and often made connections to other categorizations, such as gender or geographic context. When Du Bois (1903/1994) stated, "The problem of the twentieth century is the color line," he was concerned with the social progress of people of color, "the darker races," throughout the world in different geographic contexts and the social forces (e.g., ideas, values economic and political systems) that move and modify them. In addition, Du Bois's (1903/1994) argument that "the Negro problem in America is but the local phase of a world problem" was substantiated for me during my international travels, and reading Du Bois's work also acquainted me with the collaboration of America with England and France to develop a policy that united Western countries against African countries. Du Bois's early desire to understand the color line motivated him to explore the roots and branches of the systemic oppression of people of color worldwide. In doing so, Du Bois's efforts were fundamental to multiculturalists conducting research to understand intersectionality and how the forces of oppression (e.g., patriarchy, White privilege, abundant wealth—1%) connected and operated together. In addition, Du Bois's ways of analyzing have been useful in teaching multiculturalists the importance of remaining focused on the intersection of the legacy of enslavement and colonialism to modern-day racism and microaggression, including other systems of subordination along with White privilege.

Conclusion

In 1915a, Du Bois argued that the concept of race was that: "'Color' came into the world's thought synonymous with inferiority" (p. 709). It became, as Karenga (2002) argues, a designation of devaluation, degradation, and domination. Stripped of all its pseudoscientific claims, race is essentially a sociobiological category used to assign human worth and social status using Whites as the paradigm or standard. Multiculturalists argue that education needs to be restructured to ensure that *all* students acquire the knowledge, skills, and disposition to flourish in a racially, ethnically, socioeconomically, and culturally diverse nation and world. Multiculturalists' beliefs are consistent with Du Bois's (1904), as Saari (2009) contends: The "problem" people in marginalized groups are grounded in structures that can be changed, thus enabling multiculturalists, as Du Bois did, to propose change and reform. Du Bois (1903/1994) said to his readers in *The Souls of Black Folk*,

> Herein lie buried many things which if read with patience may show the strange meaning of being black here in the dawning of the Twentieth Century. This meaning is not without interest to you, Gentle Reader; for the problem of the Twentieth Century is the problem of the color-line.
>
> (p. v)

Multiculturalists are the "Gentle Reader," who, like Du Bois, choose to attack, deconstruct, and reconstruct the ideology, policy, and practice that ignored, misrepresented, or lied about enslavement, the "Trail of Tears," genocide, immigrants from Asia and Mexico, and the inferiority of Black and Brown children. Multiculturalists chose to offer a different path to people who are a *problem*. Multiculturalists, like Du Bois, argue for the completion of the democratic project and see hope in America's future. Du Bois (1903/1994) invited Americans "to be a co-worker in the kingdom of culture" (p. 3). Multiculturalists have taken the lit torch Du Bois passed forward and will continue in the struggle that his generation took from previous scholars such as Fredrick Douglass, Alexander Crummell, Anna Julia Cooper, Carter G. Woodson, and others.

References

ADA National Network (1990). What Is the American Disabilities Act (ADA)? Available online: https://adata.org/learn-about-ada (accessed 27 October 2016).

Bowles, S., & Gintis, H. (1976). *Schooling in capitalist America: Educational reform and contradictions of economic life*. New York: Basic Books.

Bracey, J. (n.d.). How Racism Harms White Americans. Available online: www.mediaed.org/transcripts/How-Racism-Harms-White-Americans-Transcript.pdf (accessed 1 December 2016).

Center for Public Education (2012). The United States of Education: The Changing Demographics of the United States and Their Schools. Available online: www.centerforpubliceducation.org/You-May-Also-Be-Interested-In-landing-page-level/Organizing-a-School-YMABI/The-United-States-of-education-The-changing-demographics-of-the-United-States-and-their-schools.html (accessed 28 April 2016).

Coleman, L. (2017). The Badass Wife of W. E. B. Du Bois. Available online: www.ozy.com/flashback/the-badass-wife-of-web-du-bois/62667 (accessed 18 February 2017).

Cooper, A. J. (1892). *A voice from the South*. New York: Oxford University Press.

Du Bois, W. E. B. (1891). A Constructive Critique of Wage Theory: An Essay on the Present State of Economic Theory in Regard to Wages. Available online: www.worldcat.org/title/constructive-critique-of-wage-theory-an-essay-on-the-present-state-of-economic-theory-in-regard-to-wages/oclc/77004428 (accessed 7 May 2017).

Du Bois, W. E. B. (1899). *The Philadelphia Negro*. Philadelphia: University of Pennsylvania Press.

Du Bois, W. E. B. (1920). Darkwater. NY: Dover. p. 78.

Du Bois, W. E. B. (1903/1994). *The souls of black folk*. New York: Dover.

Du Bois, W. E. B. (1906). An Address to the Country. Available online: www.american-historama.org/1913-1928-ww1-prohibition-era/niagara-movement-speech.htm (accessed 5 January 2017).

Du Bois, W. E. B. (1910). The races in conference. In Meyer Weinberg (Ed.) (1970), *A Reader: W. E. B. Du Bois* (pp. 407–408). New York: Joanna Cotier Books.

Du Bois, W. E. B. (1915a). The African Roots of War. *The Atlantic Monthly*, 115(5), May, 707–714.

Du Bois, W. E. B. (1915b). Woman Suffrage. *The Crisis*, 29–30. Available online: www.hartford-hwp.com/archives/45a/164.html (accessed 6 April 2016).

Du Bois, W. E. B. (1920). *Darkwater: Voices from within the veil*, New York: Harcourt, Brace.

Du Bois, W. E. B. (1921, August). The class struggle. Opinion. *The Crisis*, 22(4), 151. Available online: www.marxists.org/history/usa/workers/civil-rights/crisis/0800-crisis-v22n04-w130.pdf (accessed 15 December 2016).

Du Bois, W. E. B. (1926). Criteria of Negro Art. *The Crisis*, October, 290–297.

Du Bois, W. E. B. (1935a). *Black reconstruction*. New York: Harcourt, Brace and Company.

Du Bois, W. E. B. (1935b). *Does the negro need separate schools?* Washington, DC: Howard University Press.

Du Bois, W. E. B. (1947). An Appeal to the World: A Statement of Denial of Human Rights to Minorities in the Case of Citizens of Negro Descent in the United States of America and an Appeal to the United Nations for Redress. Available online: www.blackpast.org/1947-w-e-b-dubois-appeal-world-statement-denial-human-rights-minorities-case-citizens-n (accessed 23 April 2016).

Du Bois, W. E. B. (1952). *The Negro and the Warsaw Ghetto*. New York: Orthodox Jewish Congregations of America.

Friedman, T. L. (2005). *The world is flat: A brief history of twenty-first century*. New York: Farrar, Straus and Giroux.

Gordon, M. M. (1949). Social Class in American Sociology. *American Journal of Sociology*, 55(3), 262–268.

Grant, C. A., Brown, K. D., and Brown, A. L. (2016). *Black intellectual thought in education*. New York: Routledge.

Green, D. S. and Smith, E. (1983). W. E. B. Du Bois and the concepts of race and class. *Phylon*, 44(4), 262–272.

Griffin, F. J. (2000). Black feminists and Du Bois: Respectability, protection and beyond. *Annals of the American Academy of Political and Social Science*, Vol. 568, The Study of African American Problems: W. E. B. Du Bois's Agenda, Then and Now. March, pp. 28–40. Available online: http://users.clas.ufl.edu/marilynm/theorizing_black_america_syllabus_files/black_feminist_and_dubois.pdf (accessed 6 April 2016).

Guy-Sheftall, B. (1990). *Daughters of sorrow: Attitudes toward black women, 1880–1920*. Pittsburg: Carson.

James, J. (1997). Transcending the Talented Tenth: Black Leaders and American Intellectuals. Available online: www.hartford-hwp.com/archives/45a/426.html (accessed 6 January 2016).

Johnson, A. (2016). Act 10 impact on public education muted, study says. Milwaukee Wisconsin *Journal Sentinel*. Available online: http://archive.jsonline.com/news/education/act-10-impact-on-public-education-muted-study-says-b99748306z1-383870 (accessed 3 January 2017).

Karenga, M. (2002). *Introduction to black studies*, 3rd ed. Los Angeles: University of Sankore Press.

Karenga, M. (2003/2010). Du Bois and the question of the color line: Race and class in the age of globalization. Journal of Socialism and Democracy, 17, 1 141–160. www.tandfonline.com/doi/abs/10.1080/08854300308428346. 3/1/17.

Rampel, C. (December 23, 2016). Why the white working class votes against itself? www.washingtonpost.com/opinions/why-the-white-workinl, C. (December 22, 2016). Washington Post. Accessed 3/15/17.

Saari, M. M. (2009). W. E. B. Du Bois' and the Sociology of the African American Family: North Carolina Central University. *Sociation Today*, 7(1). Available online: www.ncsociology.org/sociationtoday/dubois/fam.htm (accessed 16 April 2016).

Sdonline (2011). Du Bois' and the Question of the Color Line: Race and Class in the Age of Globalization. Available online: http://sdonline.org/33/du-bois-and-the-question-of-the-color-line-race-and-class-in-the-age-of-globalization (accessed 18 April 2016).

Truth, S. (1851). *Ain't I a woman? Modern history sourcebook*. Bronx, NY: Fordham University. Available online: http://legacy.fordham.edu/halsall/mod/sojtruth-woman.asp (accessed 30 April 2016).

Washington, M. H. (1892). Introduction. In A. J. Cooper (Ed., 1982). *A voice from the South, by a black woman from the South* (pp. xxvii–liv). Xenia, Ohio: The Aldine Priniting House.

Washington, M. H. (1988). "Introduction to A Voice from the South by Anna Julia Cooper in the Schomburg Library of Nineteenth-Century Black Women Writers." New York: Oxford University Press.

Zorigian, K., & Job, J. (2015). *Minority representation in special education classrooms*. Learn, NC: Available online: www.learnnc.org/lp/pages/6799 (accessed 27 October 2016).

4

RESEARCH AND ARGUMENTS: AGAINST THE COLOR LINE

Du Bois had a great deal to say about the schooling of Black children and the education of Black people when he spoke and wrote during the first half of the 1900s that is still fresh in today's world. Du Bois's thesis in the late 1800s was education is Black people's vehicle to full citizenship and both true freedom and liberty. Over the years, Du Bois came to see, as Black people see today, that education, as crucial as it is for social uplift, must be joined with other social/civic strategies: protests, politics, experiential learning/participation, and community building in order to disrupt White power and privilege and establish an equal playing field.

Over the course of 60 years (1899–1959), Du Bois offered arguments to support and flesh out his thesis for Black equality and respect for Black humanity, and he denounced lies of scientific racism and rebuked social Darwinist assumptions that Blacks were mentally inferior and inclined to genetic pre-dispositions, such as criminality. Du Bois's arguments against scientific racism and Whites' lies and myths about Black people included rationale(s) based on sociological and scientific data analysis, examination of US social and political policy and practices, and his personal experiences as well as those of other Blacks. Du Bois argued that racism, imperialism, economic and social discrimination, disenfranchisement, and social Darwinism worked collectively against Blacks and other people of color for one major purpose: WHITE POWER, PRIVILEGE AND CAPITAL! Du Bois pointed out that Whiteness was a nineteenth- and twentieth-century idea created to establish a White racial hierarchy throughout the world in order that people with the "chosen"/superior skin color could exploit those whose skin was not white. I return again to the statement I have used before by Du Bois that needs to be said and acted on often in our current world of "hidden figures,"—people who remain hidden because of racism and sexism:

> I do not laugh. I am quite straight-faced as I ask soberly: "But what on earth is whiteness that one should so desire it?" Then always, somehow, some way, silently but clearly, I am given to understand that whiteness is the ownership of the earth forever and ever, Amen!
> (Du Bois 1920, p. 18)

Over the past 43 years, my work has benefited both theoretically and practically from Du Bois's scholarship and social advocacy. I have found academic delight in Du Bois's poetic and sobering insights, his cryptic analytical comments, and his modeling to not hesitate to think big thoughts. I have been encouraged to take a second look at problems and issues because of the way he wrote about how his ideas evolved, and, more importantly, I have gained valuable knowledge and understanding from the ways Du Bois framed and contextualized his arguments, in the moment, historically, geographically, and with an eye toward the future. In addition, my work has benefited from Du Bois's continued presence on the academic and social/civic/community stage. Du Bois's work reminds scholars and teachers, such as myself, to never fear, speak "truth to power," and, as Du Bois argues, expose evil and seek Beauty for Beauty to set the world right.

In this chapter, I discuss how Du Bois's thesis and arguments on education influenced my thinking about three areas in education where my scholarship over the years has focused: school segregation, curriculum/instructional materials, and education in urban spaces. In all three areas, the humanity of the Black child, youth, and adult was my focus.

School Segregation, Yesterday and Today: Arguments Are Mostly the Same

Yellow school buses in the morning transporting Black, Brown, and White children to school has been an American norm and welcomed way of life for decades. Norman Rockwell and other artists have illustrated this American norm on the covers of magazines and pages of newspapers over the years. Thus, as I often argued in the 1970s and 1980s,

> it is not the bus. The bus is an American way of life, the vehicle that carries children to school to pursue the American dream, including learning how to be good citizens. Instead, I argued, the school segregation/desegregation argument is about White racial antagonism toward the Black children on the bus and in the school— antagonism manifested to maintain a false narrative of White superiority and Black inferiority.

Racial segregation as a legal denial of equality based on skin color was firmly in place in the United States until the 1960s. In the North, while Blacks like my parents could cast their ballots, the schools their children attended were segregated. Ballot casting did not mean freedom from school segregation. *Brown v. Board of Education*, the Supreme Court landmark case, it should be noted, was brought forth in the northern state of Kansas and not a southern state. The decision to bring the case from a northern state underscored the struggle against racism Blacks in the North faced constantly, and it underscored the poor quality of education Black students received.

In 1972, as a Black and a newly minted PhD, I was thrown into the forced busing for racial integration battle that had become white-hot across the United States. Editors of education journals had the names of only a few Black scholars to write a journal article on their rolodex. I can't say I always welcomed those opportunities to speak out, but I never backed away. I was learning to "speak truth to power" on a national stage. I saw failure to desegregate schools in a larger context than schooling. School desegregation revealed a major fault line in American democracy and previous actions by presidents, Congress, and others had allowed the veil to remain in place and White supremacy to remain steadfast.

During the 1970s and 1980s, robust opposition to busing for racial integration took place in both the Black and White communities. Opposition caused some on both sides to ask the question Du Bois asked in 1935: "Does the Negro Need Separate Schools?" In the White community, resistance to busing centered on Whites not wanting Blacks in *their* schools and Blacks not wanting to leave *their* communities to attend schools in White communities. Busing for racial desegregation raised many pro and con questions in the Black community. On the pro side, students who attended schools under a court-ordered desegregation plan were more likely to graduate, attend college, and earn more money than Black students who attended segregated schools (Johnson, 2014). Kirp (2012) reports the achievement gap between Black and White students also declined significantly during the height of court-ordered desegregation. That said, Kirp (2012) notes that research shows that the results came about not simply by mixing races, but they were also connected to the shift in resources that came with integrating students of different races and economic classes.

The other side of the desegregation debates had its points. Although most, if not all, Blacks cheered in 1954 when *Brown* became the law of the land, not all Blacks wanted to integrate with Whites or go to schools or colleges with them. Some Blacks spoke out against desegregation because it fractured the Black community and disrupted Black "striving." Bronzeville, Chicago, for example, was a tight-knit and pretty much self-sustaining community when I grew up. It had a Black hospital, doctors, banks, lawyers, car repair shops, plumbers, electricians, insurance companies, and schools. However, middle-class Blacks in the 1960s and 1970s left their home communities, "moving on up." In doing so, they left their economically challenged, less educated Black brothers and sisters behind. Some Blacks argued that the notion of being around White people added value to the flourishing of Blacks was a myth, and they said another myth was that Black students in predominantly Black schools do not perform as well (McAuliffe, 2013). In both the Black and White communities, viewpoints changed and sometimes would change again.

As I noted in Chapter 3, Du Bois had early optimism about the integration of Blacks and Whites in public schools, but his optimism fluctuated because of the stubbornness of Whites to integrate. Du Bois initially argued for integration when he was opposing Booker T. Washington's accommodation stance in 1895. However, also in 1897, Du Bois pushed back on Fredrick Douglass's argument of Black and White integration, and again, later, in 1897, in the "Conservation of Races," Du Bois raised numerous significant questions about race as Black people moved forward and offered numerous powerful statements to Blacks about their race and their responsibility to their race. All of Du Bois's questions and statements were/are pertinent to their schooling/education. Du Bois stated,

> It is necessary . . . in guiding our future development, that . . . we rise above the pressing, but smaller questions of separate schools and cars, wage-discrimination and lynch law, to survey the whole questions of race in human philosophy and [go to the] . . . large lines of policy . . . to form our guiding lines and boundaries.
>
> (p. 1)

Du Bois then asked,

> What, after all, am I? Am I an American or am I a Negro? Can I be both? Or is it my duty to cease to be a Negro as soon as possible and be an American? If I strive as a Negro, am I not perpetuating the very cleft that threatens and separates Black and White America? Is not my only possible practical aim the subduction of all that is Negro in me to the American? Does my black blood place upon me any more obligation to assert my nationality than German, or Irish or Italian blood would?
>
> (p. 4)

Du Bois responded to his own question as he often did: "It is such incessant self-questioning and the hesitation that arises from it, that is making the present period a time of vacillation and contradiction for the American Negro" (p. 4).

From 1897 onward, for several decades, Du Bois agonized over the integration question. White resistance to integration was strong. The more than 300 years of Western empirical and scientific inquiry to support White supremacy was deeply embedded in the attitude and behavior of Whites. Du Bois could see that Whites did not want Blacks to receive equal treatment. Whites wanted to maintain their power and privilege and be constructed as superior. Again, in 1926, Du Bois stated Black people's case: "We want to be Americans, full-fledged Americans, with all the rights of American citizens" (p. 1), but added that some measure of Black "self-segregation" could bolster Black independence and culture. However, in 1934, Du Bois, arguably, had reached his limit. Fed up with the failure of racial integration to take place, as he observed the championing of "evolutionary theories, pseudoscientific literature in both social and natural science on black biological, psychological, and intellectual inferiority grow in volume, intensity and influence" (Byrd and Clayton, 2001, p. 195) and the movement from paternalistic racism (racism related to enslavement) to competitive racism (dishonest competitors for scarce resources; see Ven den Berghe (1967), Du Bois argued that Blacks should develop their own economic and political system independent of White help and support. In an essay entitled "A Negro Nation within a Nation," Du Bois laid out a compelling case against White America's refusal to adhere to the fundamental principles of democracy and called attention to the denial of education to Black children, the lynching and burning of Blacks, the unjustifiable arrests and convictions, and the job losses and unavailability because of processes of exclusion instead of inclusion. Du Bois (1934) concluded,

> The colored people of America are coming to face the fact quite calmly that most white Americans do not like them, and are planning neither for their survival, nor for their definite future if it involves free, self-assertive modern manhood.

The following year, 1935, Du Bois, even less hopeful that integrated schooling would take place, argued that Black children needed separate schools "just as far as they are necessary for the proper education of the Negro race" (p. 2). Also, Du Bois argued that if the attitude of Whites remains racially biased, Negroes would need to further increase the number of separate schools to go along with the increasing number of Blacks desirous to attend school. In conclusion, Du Bois (1935) stated, "Theoretically, the Negro needs neither segregated schools nor mixed schools. What he needs is Education" (p. 9). Du Bois's statement that what Black students need "is education" remains just as valid today, if not more so, as it did 80 plus years ago, and Du Bois's idea of education for Blacks would at least do two things: "teach life" and "develop power and ideal."

Today, the second decade of the twenty-first century, an increasing number of Blacks, especially younger Blacks, are believing, as Du Bois came to believe, that most White Americans do not like them, and they are not going to change their racist beliefs and attitudes. Whites' racist beliefs and attitudes are demonstrated in the way(s) Blacks are treated in US public schools. Suspensions, inexperienced teachers and segregation is what many Black students face in schools. Recent federal data reports Black students are nearly four times as likely as their White classmates to be suspended from school (Khan, 2016, p. 1). In addition, Toppo (2016) reports that US Education Secretary John King said, "From gifted-and-talented programs to teacher experience to advanced science and math courses . . . schools that enroll large numbers of minority students are unequal in nearly every way" (p. 1). Secretary King added that 11% of Black students and 9% of Latino students are taught by beginning/inexperienced teachers in comparison to 5% of White students and 4% of Asian students, which lays bare the USA's systemic failure to educate all students equally.

According to the current research and popular literature on school desegregation/integration, "It's not uncommon to find public schools across the country with students isolated by race and income" (Anderson, 2016, p. 1). Whereas, the *Atlantic* article written by Anderson (2016) notes that the latest research shows hopeful trends as more school districts pursue promising integration patterns for both students of color and Whites, the article also points out that "research does not reveal how to bridge the gap between belief and action" (p. 1), and the reality of integrated schools lags. Of the "more than 15,000 school districts in the U.S., some 50 million students in K–12 schools, and 92 percent of students remain in racially and socioeconomically homogenous schools" (Anderson, 2016, p. 2). Although the push for integrated schools continues as better test scores, increased college attendance, and improved critical-thinking skills are held up as the result of integrated schools, it is also argued that such positive findings are more the result of students attending schools where there are sufficient high-quality human and material resources, along with the economic uplift of the students' families. Moreover, Semuels (2015) writing in the *Atlantic* reports Black-White segregation is becoming more pronounced in many US neighborhoods. Semuels (2015) contends that segregation practices such as "white flight, exclusionary zoning, and outright prejudice, are continuing to create black areas and white areas, but this time around, those areas exist in both the cities and suburbs" (p. 1). In addition, Black youth today are acutely aware of the hardship and violence that the youth of the 1950s and 1960s endured during school desegregation in the North and the South. Today's Black youth know that Black students were spit on, poked, clubbed, and cursed. Furthermore, they see that racist social situation(s)—personal and institutional—in America keep repeating (e.g., mass killing of Black men and women, Black people suffering, afraid to leaves their homes, local schools closing while White people play and use coded language to "blame the victim"). In addition, the social and political media often portray Blacks as "outside the system of reality" (Baldwin, 2017). In other words, Black youth argue that when a group of people—White people—have enslaved, lynched, segregated, and lied about you, they don't like you! Thus when Black youth experience racial microaggressions on college campuses and as they go about their daily business in the public spaces across the country, they know that Du Bois's observation about White's attitudes toward Blacks has changed only somewhat for the better, and to some that is a debatable issue.

Perhaps the most divisive argument that Du Bois had to challenge regarding the education of Black youth, and one we continue today, is that White people's intelligence is superior to Black people's. Du Bois challenged the White superiority trope throughout his life, changing and adding to his argument as he discovered supportive information. That White people are one standard deviation above Black people in intelligence has never been completely laid to rest, although the clamor about it has quieted down at times. In a recent book titled *The Long Crusade: Profiles in Education Reform* by Raymond Wolters (2014), the author of *Du Bois and His Rivals* has reactivated the discussion. Wolters (2014) analyzes and critiques different educational reform efforts to close the Black-White achievement gap. Wolters contends that the educational reform efforts that grew out of the *Brown* decision to desegregate schools and to close the Black-White achievement gap are a "history of failures." Wolters (2014) claims "cultural explanations," "additional school funding," "court ordered busing," "teachers caring for Black students," "culturally relevant/responsive curriculum," and "celebrated graduates of Teach for America" have all failed to close the Black-White achievement gap. Wolters (2014) argues that proposals by progressives (e.g., Jonathan Kozol, 1967, 1991; Howard Gardner, *Multiple Intelligences*; Ted Sizer, *Phillips Academy*), "back to the basic" reformers (e.g., E. D. Hirsch, *Cultural Literacy*, Robert Slavin), and current reformers (e.g., Wendy Kopp, Teach for America) have failed to close the achievement gap. Instead, Wolters, ignoring the critiques of each of these examples, argues that it would be wiser to acknowledge that the IQ data gathered from questionable, biased tests has been consistent for decades: Black students are one standard deviation off from White students. Reading Wolters's (2014) thesis that "biology" is more influential than "culture," I said, "Here we go again" to myself. Racism in its many shapes and forms continues to travel across the decades. That time it was being touted by a so-called racial realist who is doing nothing more than promoting intellectual racism. Du Bois (1920) stated in "Souls of White Folk":

> They [White people] deny my right to live and be and call me mis-birth! My word is to them mere bitterness and my soul, pessimism.

> And yet as they preach and strut and shout and threaten, crouch-
> ing as they clutch at rags of facts and fancies to hide their naked-
> ness, they go twisting, flying by my tired eyes and I see them ever
> stripped—ugly, human.

(p. 17)

Next, I went to the debate "Should the Negro be Encouraged to Cultural Equality?" (see Taylor, 1981) between The-
odore Lothrop Stoddard, a Harvard PhD, and Du Bois in my
home town of Chicago. Stoddard's thesis was:

> [O]ur America is a White America. . . . And the overwhelming weight
> of both historical and scientific evidence shows that only so long as
> the American people remain white will its institutions, ideals and
> culture continue to fit the temperament of its inhabitants—and
> hence continue to endure.

(Taylor, 1981, p. 1)

Stoddard, Taylor (1912, p. 1) writes, had excellent reason to celebrate the clarity of his perceptions and the self-
evidence of his conclusions. Quite literally, he had it on the
best authority that the "leading figures in American social
science . . . biologists, psychologists, and sociologist pro-
claimed with one voice the inherent and immutable inferiority of the Black race." Du Bois argued that scientific racism
was a closed system—as are many of the proposed solutions
to close the Black-White achievement gap—supported by
weak methodology and perpetuated by biased researchers
(Taylor, 1981).

Reviewing the claims of racial superiority by proponents
of social Darwinism has changed over the years, but they per-
sisted. In the early decades of the 1900s, Du Bois challenged

racial antagonism between Black and Whites based on several claims that have been proven false including that there was an instinctive repulsion between Black and White, Blacks were deteriorating because of poor health, and Blacks were instinctive rapists caught up in an overpowering desire for White women. Regarding the claims, all of which seem ludicrous in a 2017 light, Du Bois pointed out, regarding the first one, that Black and White children play together willingly, and today, we see on college campuses and in shopping malls Blacks and Whites who not only play together but also live together. Regarding the second claim, according to BlackDemographics.com,

> The last census count during slavery in 1860 counted 4,441,830 African Americans, of which 89% were slave, by 1900 the Black population grew to more than 8 million and more than doubled every 50-year period since reaching 42 million by 2010.

The social Darwinist's statement about the Blacks deteriorating was another lie to promote the neglect of Black humanity. Furthermore, according to Byrd and Clayton (2001) Blacks have withstood racism in medicine that is at least 2,500 years old. With the third claim, Taylor (1912, p. 456) caused a provoked Du Bois to state,

> For a generation, we black folks have been the sexual scape-goats for white American filth in literature and lynching. Every time a black man commits a crime, the story is garnished and embellished by unbelievable sadism in order to make a beast out of the criminal. It is not enough that a black man robs or kills or fights. No! In addition to that, the world must be made to believe him a wild beast of such inconceivable and abnormal appetites that he turns from

red force and white anger to filthy lust. No proof is asked for such incredible lies.

(The Crisis, October, 1930, p. 353)

Du Bois (1930) added that only 19% of Blacks lynched had been accused of rape and much fewer convicted.

Returning to Wolters's (2014) critique of the educational reform efforts, I wondered if the critiques, as insightful as they were, but not something that could be founded in the education literature, were not a "straw man." Each of the reform efforts that Wolters discusses to close the Black-White achievement gap arguably have merit, but individually, and in some cases collectively, they are not enough to do away with 500 years of enslavement, segregation, Jim Crow, poor schooling for Blacks, and living in poor economic conditions. Furthermore, I contend, borrowing from Terry (1970; quoted in Byrd and Clayton, 2001), that "power" is the unfair distribution or disproportional capacity of Whites to make and enforce decisions, differential control of resources such as money education, information and political influence by Whites; the establishment of societal standards by Whites, and the defining of the problem and prescribing the solution by Whites that are not fully considered when challenging that Black-White achievement must be considered.

Du Bois would come back to the question of desegregation and integration throughout his life, and his understanding of and challenges to the "race concept" would grow as he fought against the White superiority and Black inferiority thesis. Although many of the supportive arguments used by Whites to show Blacks' inferiority to Whites are based on racial prejudice grounded in "ignorance and a deep-rooted rational and irrational beliefs among whites" (Olson, 2005,

p. 2), they are quickly forgotten by Whites as they chase the newest idea or rationale to argue that they are superior to Blacks.

Curriculum: Reinforcing the Color Line

> I believe in pride of race and lineage and self—in pride of self so deep as to scorn injustice to other selves.
>
> (Du Bois, 1920, p. 3)

In my early research, starting with class projects, dissertation, and my first published article, I was addressing the color line and discussing the racism perpetrated on Black children who lived behind the veil. Little did I know that my criticism of science textbooks, curriculum, and instructional materials for race, social class, and gender bias when I was teaching at Wadsworth Elementary School in Chicago would become the first line of my research and scholarship. As I discussed in Chapter 2, I refused to use the science textbooks assigned to my class and was told by my principal, Mr. Pearl, that since I knew science, I should just use supplemental materials. I was vexed by Mr. Pearl's statement because it was expressed flippantly, but more so because it disrespected my students and underscored what Du Bois (1935) argued, which is that Blacks needed contact with school officials on the "basis of perfect social equality" (p. 2). The disrespect of Black humanity in the textbooks has a long history that is difficult to eliminate. Bob Peterson, founding editor of *Rethinking School*, in 1998, reported,

> I've been a member of a district committee that adopts social-studies textbooks for kindergarten through fifth grade. I have not found even one reference to race or racism in the four U.S. history textbooks

under consideration for fifth grade. . . . When I mentioned to one textbook company representative that there was no reference to race or racism in his U.S. history textbook, he responded, "Darn, that's interesting. I hadn't noticed that before."

(p. 1)

Presently, the demographic shift notwithstanding, much of the reading and curriculum materials for students remains trapped in a 1930s time warp that was expressed in a 1965 article in the *Saturday Review*: "The All-White World of Children's Books." Over the past years, the rise in immigration, increase in birth rates among Latino women, growth in the number of disabled students mainstreamed into general classrooms, and students not hiding their sexual orientation has changed public school classrooms. "In 2008, the Census Bureau reported, elementary and high school students today are more diverse by race and Hispanic origin than the Baby Boom generation of students" (Center for Public Education, 2012, p. 4). This demographic shift, along with the movement away from the use of standard textbooks in schools calls for reading and curriculum materials that are multicultural, inclusive, and free of gender bias. However, as Pirofski (2015) reports, such reading and curriculum materials are simply not available, "and our literary canon seems bereft of books depicting minorities, African Americans, disabled, and non-sexist literary characters (p. 1). Similarly, Teaching for Change (2015) contends,

The diversity gap in children's books and the publishing industry is wide and in the past 20 years has not significantly changed. Only 14% of children's books published in 2014 were by or about people of color and Native Americans.

(p. 1)

Pirpfski (2015), Teaching for Change (2015), and other studies that report there is an absence of diverse reading and curriculum materials for Black students today are similar to the findings of Du Bois in the twentieth century. From reading Du Bois, I imagined he queried, "Where do Black children learn about the beauty of their Blackness?," "Where do Black people learn about their history and culture in the United States and the global society?," and "Where do Black children learn about democracy?"

Du Bois was a pioneer in arguing for the full blossom of democracy for Blacks and against the racial bias in textbooks and other news and entertainment media. Du Bois saw the classroom and the curriculum materials, therein, as a path to learning and enlightenment and individual and collective liberty of Blacks. Du Bois (1924) believed that American democracy crippled itself by distorting, omitting, and inaccurately reporting the story of Blacks and their gifts to America. In the *Gift of Black Folks*, Du Bois (1924) argued that it was the Negro who made America understand democracy: the country's political system that advocates human rights of all citizens and that all citizens should have a say in everything that affects their lives regardless of their race or skin color. Du Bois (1924) posits:

> The democracy established in America in the eighteenth century was not designed to be, a democracy of the masses of men and it was thus singularly easy for people to fail to see the incongruity of democracy and slavery. It was the Negro himself who forced consideration of this incongruity, who made emancipation inevitable and made the modern world at least consider if not wholly accept the idea of a democracy including men of all races and colors.

> (p. 139)

In 1935, Du Bois spoke about the potential of American democracy when Blacks are fully involved and their humanity is prized. The same year Carter G. Woodson established Negro History Week, Du Bois asked Blacks, "Do we simply want to be American?" Du Bois (1935) answered, "We who are dark can see America in a way that white Americans cannot . . . . a world where men know, where men create, where they realize themselves and where they enjoy life" (p. 1). Du Bois was forever optimistic about what knowledge could do for people who prized democracy and who respected the humanity in each other. He believed that if we read and studied about each other, we would have a bright future. Du Bois (1940a) stated,

> As we grow . . . let us take the first opportunity of studying the histories and cultures of Asia, Australia, and the early history and culture of America and let us expand the study we now attempt to make of the history and culture of Africa, to the end that our work in the social sciences may present the relevant past, not to minds living in the past but to the minds of those who will live and shape the world of the future.

Du Bois's argument that the problem of the color line was not simply a national or personal question, but one that needed to be considered within a larger world aspect of time and space, broaden my observation and analysis of curriculum. In 1915, Du Bois wrote *The Negro.* The book heightened my interest in curriculum and instructional research on a global level. In *The Negro*, Du Bois chronicled the history of African peoples and their descendants in various places in the world. Du Bois's Pan-African argument gave me both knowledge and greater appreciation of the contributions of Blacks worldwide. *The Negro* gave attention to cultural contributions, historical achievements, and challenges faced by Blacks in different regions of the world. *The Negro* discussed the African Diaspora, enslaved people in the United States, and critiqued Reconstruction. Also, in *Dusk of Dawn*, Du Bois (1940a) spoke to Blacks about a common bond, a historical connection: the color line/veil. Du Bois stated,

> One thing is sure and that is the fact that since the fifteenth century these ancestors of mine and their descendants have had a common history; have suffered a common disaster . . . the real essence of this kinship is its social heritage of slavery; the discrimination and insult; and this heritage binds together not simply the children of Africa, but extends through yellow Asia and into the South Seas.
>
> (p. 8)

When I supervised UW teacher candidates who were doing their student teaching in England (1970–1980), and when I was a Fulbright Scholar in 1982 and had the opportunity to travel and visit schools throughout Europe, I inquired of teachers and other educators about their curriculum materials. I would ask, How are the minoritized people in the country portrayed? How are women and girls represented? What can you, as teachers, teach and openly discuss and what can't you? How is social class depicted? Are there suggestions in textbooks to promote discussions on how to improve the role of the government to better serve all people? In addition, my two schoolchildren, Carl (middle school) and Alicia (primary school), often traveled with me. They attended school in England, which made my access to schoolbooks and other curriculum materials easy. At the time of my Fulbright fellowship in 1982, Du Bois's argument that race is sociological and not based in biology rarely found its way into school textbooks and other forms of narratives in the United States and places where I traveled in Europe.

Several of my graduate students from different countries have found this research inviting and have taken part in it. However, a few hesitate to be publicly connected to this work. Such hesitation from my graduate students has further opened my eyes to the oppression of people because of their national origin, gender, religion, sexual orientation, and social class. Du Bois's attention to the color line at the international level called my attention to the gross inequities of power, domination, and suppression by Whites on people of color throughout the world and how White superiority is transmitted through school curriculum, teaching practices, and social mediums.

The Brownies' Books: Tearing Away the Veil

> There is No Place for Black Children in This World.
>
> (Du Bois, 1920, p. 202)

Five years after writing *The Negro*, Du Bois, Augustus Granville Dill, and Jessie Redmon Fauset founded *The Brownies' Books* (1920–1922), which were devoted to children and youth between the ages of 6 and 16. Before Du Bois started publishing *The Brownies' Books*, each year, *The Crisis* would feature an issue called "Children's Number," dedicated to Black children. The issue would feature a variety of literature, songs, art, and games mostly written or created by Blacks. In addition, Du Bois would write a column that caringly introduced Black children to the serious and painful side of being Black in America. Du Bois included information on lynchings and other violence perpetuated against Blacks. Du Bois knew that Black children heard about and possibly saw these horrors of violence committed against Blacks, so he wanted to speak to them in ways that would give them hope, help them feel less afraid, and tell them about the beauty of their humanity. Indicative of Du Bois's respect for all humanity, he stated in *The Crisis* before the inaugural issue of *The Brownies' Books* in January 1920 that they were "designed for all children, but especially for ours" (p. 10). The publication of *The Brownies' Books* for "the children of the sun," a phrase used to describe the primary audience, was in circulation for two years.

As a child, I discovered some back issues of *The Brownies' Books* in my home. I read them from cover to cover. I came to understand what reading *Brownies' Books* taught children about the nobleness of their humanity: they were not invisible; the history of their culture was rich and prideful, and they were beautiful. Du Bois (1919) identified seven goals for *Brownie Books*:

> To make colored children realize that being "colored" is a normal, beautiful thing.
>
> To make them familiar with the history and achievements of the Negro race.
>
> To make them know that other colored children have grown into beautiful, useful and famous persons.
>
> To teach them a delicate code of honor and action in their relations with white children.
>
> To turn their little hurts and resentments into emulation, ambition and love of their homes and companions.
>
> To point out the best amusements and joys and worth-while things of life.
>
> To inspire them to prepare for definite occupations and duties with a broad spirit of sacrifice.

(p. 286)

Du Bois (1919) wrote prior to the first publication of *The Brownies' Books*, "Heretofore the education of the Negro child had been too much in terms of Whites. All through school life his [her] text-books contain much about white people and little or nothing about his [her] own race" (p. 2). Whenever Du Bois wrote about "children of the sun," his love, deep caring, and advocacy for them was clear. Du Bois did not want Black children to remain invisible or see themselves as invisible. Instead, through *The Brownies' Books* and his other work, Du Bois said to Black children that they were normal and beautiful, should learn their history, and develop their intellectual and artistic gifts.

In 1904, Du Bois wrote,

> I believe the training of children, black even as white; the leading out of little souls into the green pastures and the cool waters, not for self or peace, but for life lit by some large vision of beauty and goodness and truth.
>
> (p. 202)

Du Bois wanted all Americans to stand up for children against the ravages of racism and a failure of American democracy to appreciate them fully and to let them know that they are the future of America. Du Bois (1904) stated, "Save the great principles of democracy and equal opportunity and fight segregation by wealth, class or race or color, not by yielding to it, but by watching, visiting and voting in all school matters" (p. 202).

Du Bois's deep and devoted caring for children was heightened with the death of his son, Burghardt, at the age of two from diphtheria. Burghardt's death arguably occurred because, in Atlanta, Georgia, medical services were not readily available to Black people. "The Passing of the First Born" in *Souls* (1903), as well as the brutality of the lynching death of Sam Hose, a Black man, devastated Du Bois and made him vividly aware of his Blackness and that those who kept the color line in place show no emotion with the death of a helpless Black child. Two paragraphs from "The Passing of the First Born" describe Du Bois's anger about the color line, living in the Veil, and his acknowledgment that Blacks will be second class for "long, long years to come."

> We could not lay him in the ground there in Georgia, for the earth there is strangely red; so we bore him away to the northward, with his flowers and his little folded hands. In vain, in vain!—for where, O God! beneath thy broad blue sky shall my dark baby rest in peace,— where Reverence dwells, and Goodness, and a Freedom that is free?
>
> (p. 155)

I often recall the grieving words by Du Bois (1903/1994) in "The Passing of the First Born," when I see Black mothers coming before the media after the deaths of their sons or daughters because of racist police behavior: "For where, O God! beneath thy broad blue sky shall my dark baby rest in peace." For both Black mothers and Du Bois, the deaths of their children symbolize the injustice and heartache that has been laid upon Blacks throughout history because of racism and the demands of White power and privilege.

Looking back, I think reading *The Brownies' Books* when I was a child planted seeds of advocacy in me for how schoolbooks should be. The characters should be inclusive of race, class, gender, and (dis)ability diversity. As I look back over my career critiquing and writing curriculum, it has been to continue the advocacy Du Bois started decades ago. The challenge

Gloria and I posed to school officials and our teacher colleagues about the race, gender, and social-class bias in curriculum was simply us climbing on the shoulders of Du Bois and believing in the statement he wrote in *The Crisis* (1919) about *The Brownies' Books*:

> It will be a thing of Joy and Beauty, dealing in Happiness, Laughter and Emulation, and designed especially for Kiddies from Six to Sixteen. It will seek to teach Universal Love and Brother hood for all little folk, black and brown and yellow and white.
>
> (p. 286)

Teaching at the Color Line

> For education among all kinds of men always has had, and always will have, an element of danger and revolution, of dissatisfaction and discontent.
>
> (Du Bois, 1903/1994, p. 35)

I begin this final section of *Du Bois and Education* as a college professor who believes that "the true college (graduate) will ever have one goal—not to earn meat but to know the end and aim of that life which meat nourishes" (Du Bois, 1903/1994, p. 70). Writing about education in urban spaces has been another focus of my research, and Du Bois's discussion of democracy and education has been valuable to my research. The urban space, particularly, Chicago's Black Belt and the Bronzeville area, is my site of intersection of historical/ cultural and geographical study of race. It is in urban areas where I believe that democracy is feeble and in need of Du Bois's theorizing on the ideologies and methodologies of race and racism.

Du Bois argues that democracy in America for Blacks is about more than the struggle to desegregate schools, Blacks' integration into US society, and being able to perform civic duties and having the rights guaranteed by the Bill of Rights. Du Bois asserted that this idea of democracy is good, but it is lacking. Democracy, Du Bois (1920) declared, is about enlightenment and learning as the gateway to individual and collective freedom and liberty. Du Bois (1920) argued,

> Democracy alone is the method of showing the whole experience of the race for the benefit of the future and if democracy tries to exclude women or Negroes or the poor or any class because of innate characteristics which do not interfere with intelligence, then that democracy cripples itself and belies its name.
>
> (p. 84)

In 1915, Du Bois issued a statement that has been meaningful to how I think about democracy and education as it relates to students of color. Du Bois stated, "A program for black people will be meaningless unless it is mediated to their ideals and their development." Central to this idea would be an education that is liberal or technical or constructed to meet the needs/challenges of Black students. Democracy and education from a Du Boisian perspective in this time of persistent segregation in schools and the failure of public schools to educate Black and Brown children, would mean Blacks and Browns having more control of the governance (e.g., policy, practice, resources) of their schools, including curriculum and employment of teachers, principals, and staff. Also, from a Du Boisian perspective, the hope would be to have racially integrated schools that include students, teachers, and other staff members, but the absolute would be to have schools where Blacks receive an education. These Du Boisian ideas on American democracy and democracy and education have served me as an ideology and an imperative. Also, from observing how Du Bois focused on both national and international issues of the color line— northern and southern racism, US politics, Pan-Africanism, treatment of Jewish people, and human rights—I saw democracy and democracy and education as part of my research agenda. In *Darkwater*, Du Bois (1920) noted democracy is not the need of a particular group, but "democracy is a method of realizing the broadest measure of justice to all human being" (p. 82).

In this final section, I thread Du Bois's attention to democracy and education through my research and analysis of education in urban spaces using CPS as my example. I thread Du Bois's attention to democracy and education through my teaching of teacher candidates at UW in order to prepare them to teach in schools in urban spaces and in smaller places such as Madison, Wisconsin. I join Du Bois and ask, "What is the meaning of progress . . . for Blacks?"

Democracy and the Color Line in Urban Spaces

Urban spaces, like the one where I grew up on the south side of Chicago, were and continue to be antithetical to the principles of democracy. The south side of Chicago is a segregated pocket of poverty space, where the racism directed toward Blacks and Latinos/as is pervasive and has always been that way. Equality and respect for Black and Brown humanity continues to represent the limits of American democracy, and in an urban space such as Chicago, where democracy is comprised and controlled by a White governing authority, the color line represents democracy failure.

Four years ago, my brother Shelby and I wrote a book titled *The Moment: Barack Obama, Jeremiah Wright and the Firestorm at Trinity United Church of Christ*. *The Moment* tells the inside story of Trinity UCC (then-Senator Obama's church) during the 2008 presidential elections and the media firestorm over his pastor, Reverend Wright. Researching and writing the second chapter, "Race, Migration, and Politics in the Windy City," led me to investigate democracy and education in the context of early twentieth-century Black life in Chicago through a Du Boisian-inspired framework and discuss it in relation to Black life in Chicago after WWII to the present day. From that analysis and discussion, I, along with several coauthors, have written several articles and chapters in books on education in urban spaces with a focus on Chicago. What follows is a brief discussion, for contextual purposes, of Black life in CPS for Black students using a Du Boisian democracy and education lens.

A Short Briefing on the Color Line in Chicago: Housing and Schools

The migration of African Americans to Chicago and other places north and west from 1915 to 1939 as they fled the South to escape lynchings and Jim Crow laws, earn a living, and taste the fruits of democracy often led to another form of racism and segregation: a denial of democracy and poor education. In Chicago, fleeing Blacks were segregated to the Black Belt: a seven-miles long and one-half mile wide area on the city's south side. For Black people, Richard Wright tells us in *12 Million Voices* that every facet of life was rough: housing, employment, schools, health, and well-being on city streets during the summer and winter. For several decades, many Blacks, who came during the Great Migration lived wherever they could find a place. They lived with friends and relatives; in storage rooms, garages, basements; and in overcrowded apartment buildings, where the rooms had been cut up into smaller one-room apartments without a bathroom and/or a kitchen.

In the late 1940s and early 1950s, the Chicago Housing Authority (CHA) begin to construct large public housing developments for Black families that complied with racist federal policy: "Neighborhood Composition Rule," "which required that the tenants of a new housing development be of the same race as the people of the area in which it was located" (Encyclopedia of Chicago, n.d.). During the mid-1950s and 1960s, the CHA built high-rise projects of 15 to 19 stories for Blacks. The projects had between 150 to 4,415 apartments. The projects, however, soon became run down, because too many people lived in a very closed space and service and upkeep, including working elevators, did not take place as needed. The projects, however, served as a way for Black ward bosses and prescient captains of the area to control the votes of the tenants. Further, the segregated projects gave Blacks false *propaganda*: you are inferior; therefore, you are kept separate from White people who are superior.

The State of Illinois outlawed school segregation in 1847; however, the statute was ignored because it didn't contain an enforcement mechanism and included loopholes that permitted school officials to do as they pleased. Schools in urban Chicago are still segregated, and over the years, city officials, as I noted in Chapter 2, have continued to resist having White students and students of color attend the same school. In schools where students of color and Whites attend together, Black and Brown students are often not in the same classrooms or assigned to the same classes with White students. Black and

Brown students have freedom to attend school, but they are not at liberty to learn in spaces with White students. Thus White students continue to be taught that freedom and liberty are one and the same and that the reason Black and Brown students are not in the same classes with them is that they are intellectually inferior. A democracy that does not give all its citizens' moral dignity and respect, Du Bois (1920) contends, will not create the America that can foster a beautiful world.

Between 1920 and 1930, the Black population in Chicago grew from 109,458 to 233,903, doubling the number of Black students in segregated schools, and the number of segregated schools rose from 6 to 26 (Homel, 1984). The present-day beliefs and arguments about the poor quality of schooling on Chicago's south and west sides, where Blacks and Browns live and attend school, can be traced back to policies and practices of the 1920s and 1930s and the attitudes of the Whites in the mayor's and school superintendent's offices (Pinderhughes, 1987). Sustar (2013) states,

> From the first attempts to steer the growing Black population into segregated schools in the 1930s to todays more sophisticated, corporate-backed "education reformers," Chicago politicians and school authorities have carried out a persistent effort to keep Black students in segregated, inferior schools. In the 1920s and 30s that meant channeling the city's booming African American population into ghettoes [on the south side].

> (p. 2)

Martin Luther King Jr., at the height of the Civil Rights Movement in 1965, argued, "Chicago was far from being the promised land." As I discussed in Chapter 2, when King came to Chicago to protest segregated housing and schools, I was teaching eighth grade science at Wadsworth, a K–8 grade Black school on the south side of the city. In some classrooms at Wadsworth, 50 or more Black children were sitting wherever they could find space. The first and second grade teachers at Wadsworth were teaching a "double shift" because of classroom overcrowding; three classrooms each of first and second grade students came to school from 8 a.m. to 11:30 a.m. and a second group of first and second graders attended school from 11:45 a.m. to 3:15 a.m. At the same time, schools in White neighborhoods, only three to five miles away, had both low student enrollment and many vacant desks. Whereas the Black students received the minimum number of contact hours necessary for the school to receive state aid, Black students' education was severely shortchanged. Black students were herded in and out, art and music classes were cut short or eliminated, and teachers had little or no time to talk with parents about their children's learning at a formative time of their young lives.

The reduced teaching time for students was not an original occurrence for Blacks at Wadsworth and in Chicago. In 1939, the *Chicago Defender* reported that "78% of Negro children spend 40% less time in school than do children outside of the colored communities in Chicago" (Knupfer, 2006, p. 12). Further, Black children not receiving equality of time in the school has a legacy that dates to Emancipation and for decades afterward. The color line in US education hangs like shackles around the neck, legs, and arms of Black children.

Gloria, my wife, was one of the three first grade teachers at the school. She told me on numerous occasions about how "double-shift" schooling was affecting the quality of education Black students received. She argued, "There's not enough time to give them the attention they really need," especially since there was no lunch hour to work with students who needed a few more minutes of instruction. It was nearly impossible to correct the overwhelmingly large stacks of papers to give students immediate feedback. Gloria and her other two colleagues often complained of being worn down. Field trips, important to growing young minds, were all but eliminated. The short school day prevented leaving the school and returning to adhere to a daily schedule. Keeanga-Yamahtta Taylor (2012) explains, by late the 1950s, Chicago was undergoing "neighborhood change." Whites were moving out of the city by the thousands, and African Americans were moving into the city by the thousands. In some neighborhoods on the south side, I saw moving vans stack up like planes over O'Hare Airport waiting to land on a holiday weekend. Whites wanted no part of living next door to Blacks, who were only searching for decent places to live and raise their families.

The CPS curriculum omitted, distorted, and reported inaccurately on the history and culture of Blacks and other people of color. The official curriculum was *propaganda* filled with lies: Black enslaved people were happy and ignorant, and Whites were the superior race. Adding to this insult, Black students were often forced to use old books previously used by White students on the city's north side and in suburbs. White superiority, power, and privilege were boldly on display in classrooms on the south side.

Many everyday folks on Chicago's south side knew of W. E. B. Du Bois. They knew about his curriculum debate with Booker T. Washington over an academic versus a vocational curriculum. Du Bois's scholarship and on-the-ground action demonstrated his ongoing effort to see to it that Blacks received a school curriculum and a life curriculum that encouraged them to challenge the role of inferiority Whites had assigned to them. In the first chapter of *Souls*, "Our Spiritual Strivings," one of my favorite essays in the book, Du Bois (1903/1994) discusses Blacks' consciousness: "'two-ness,' . . . two souls, two thoughts, two unreconciled striving, two warring ideals in one dark body" (p. 3). Here Du Bois showed the contradictory positioning of Blacks within the dominant society and their need for a democratic and multicultural curriculum—a curriculum that teaches Blacks and other students of color to see themselves as they are, not a false image of themselves manufactured by Whites. Blacks and other students of color, Du Bois argued, needed a curriculum that teaches high expectations and encourages the pursuit of goals fostered by demonstrated beliefs in Black students and other students of color. Such a curriculum is needed because the marginalization of Blacks has led to a distorted image of self and view of Blacks' place in the world.

Black men and women fleeing the South in the early 1900s dreamed of a better life in the North. They dreamed of economic uplift, through employment that paid better wages than in the South, and social and political uplift, by leaving behind Jim Crow and harsh segregationist laws. They hoped their skin color wouldn't cause them to suffer and they would be away from the "gaze of the white male" (Morrison, 1998, p. 1) However, many Blacks were greatly disappointed. White employers refused to hire Blacks. Claims of inferior mental capacity were used to keep Blacks in the lowest level jobs. Jobs in factories, foundries, and slaughterhouses came with dangerous and arduous working conditions and propagandized the inferiority thesis. Black women, including many single mothers who came to Chicago in greater numbers than men, experienced even greater hardship in the form of racism and sexism. Employers were reluctant to hire Black women. Employers argued that women can't do "men's work"; they should raise children, and they will not be a stable workforce because they will become pregnant. Another force operating against Black women's job opportunities were White women, who did not want to work alongside Black women: and although White women argued for gender equality, most did not favor racial equality. In addition, White women feared doing the same jobs as Black women would lower their status and possibly the status of the position in which they worked (Cannon, 1995). The job opportunities open to Black women were mostly as domestics. Cannon (1995) states, "The black woman began her life of freedom with no vote, no protection, and no equity of any sort. Black women, young and old were basically on their own" (p. 51)

Racism remains in Chicago as I write today. The color line is present in the form of racial profiling (CBS Chicago, 2016) and police shootings. Katie Reilly of TIME.com (2016) in Chicago revealed that "about four of every five people shot by police officers in Chicago in the past six years were African American males" (p. 1). Segregation and unequal education continue in CPS, despite the 1980 lawsuit by the US federal government against CPS for discriminating against Black and Brown students and other efforts. Additionally, since the 1990s, CPS has undergone a series of institutional reforms consistent with neoliberal ideologies for urban development. The mayor's office and businesses argued that CPS and public education is out of step for an "entrepreneurial city." Means (2008) reports that it was argued that CPS's governing system and ways of operating were old, inefficient, and corrupt, and thus incapable of providing the educational innovation needed to serve the demands of the global economy. To that end, city hall and the business community of Chicago instituted a new plan,

Renaissance 2010, "to clear the ground for corporate development through privatization and school closures" (Means, 2008, p. 2). Means (2008) contends that CPS's plan undermines education quality.

I argue that it also riles against the principals of democratic governance and marginalizes the democratic process, and in doing so, it renews and strengthens the color line. At the heart of Renaissance 2010 and Chicago becoming an entrepreneurial city was school reform grounded in deregulation and dismantling, public-private partnership, and a movement to school choice. In 2013, the mayor's office initiated the closure of 49 public schools and 61 buildings (Anthony, 2014). The schools closed predominately served Blacks and Latino students, who represent most students in CPS. The school closures affected 87% of CPS students of color (National Center for Education Statistics, 2016). Within a short period, reutilized buildings began housing an increasing number of charter schools, and the movement to charter schools brought increased segregation and fortified the color line. This neoliberal effort in the form of a "school choice movement" undercut the progressive movement that grew out of the civil rights efforts of the 1960s. It was a return to liberalism of the free market. It reduced services, wages, and benefits to Blacks struggling to soften the effects of the color line and segregated housing.

When Du Bois argued that the "problem of the twentieth is the problem of the color line," he foresaw how, what today we call "neoliberalism," would impact people of color. Du Bois understood as Tabb (2003) argues, "The damages, its causes, the interests it serves, and the way it divides the working class and undercuts the progressive movements with horrible consequences at home and abroad" (p. 1). Du Bois, writing in

The Crisis in 1893 and in his address at the first Pan-African Congress, addressed how globalization, racism, and free markets undercut multiracial inclusion, how it leads to cutting and eliminating government and local services and feeding the insatiable appetite of the very rich who live among us but not with us.

Du Bois spoke of how European governments were interested in revenue at any cost and at any people's expense. He noted how Europe "cast covetous eyes" upon the financial profit of Spain in slave trafficking in the fifteenth century, and slave trafficking came to dominate European business a century later. The Gilder Lehrman Institute of American History in a review of Eric Williams's (1944) *Capitalism and Slavery* discussed how the North and the South reaped rewards from the work and suffering of enslaved Blacks:

> In the pre-Civil War United States a stronger case can be made that slavery played a critical role in economic development. One crop, slave-grown cotton, provided over half of all US export earnings. By 1840, the South grew 60 percent of the world's cotton and provided some 70 percent of the cotton consumed by the British textile industry. Thus, slavery paid for a substantial share of the capital, iron, and manufactured goods that laid the basis for American economic growth. In addition, precisely because the South specialized in cotton production, the North developed a variety of businesses that provided services for the slave South, including textile factories, a meat processing industry, insurance companies, shippers, and cotton brokers.
>
> (p. 2)

The Chicago mayor's office and the business community "cast covetous eyes" on Black and Brown young bodies in CPS, whom they view as a way to make money with an education for profit scheme known as charter schools. I have witnessed the racist control of Black and Brown bodies throughout my life by CPS and the mayor's office; I have watched the flow of Black bodies from schools into the private prison industrial complexes. I am reminded of Du Bois's (1915) claim about Western Whites' desire to colonize Black, Brown, and Yellow people to serve their own interests, regardless of the cost to people of color. Du Bois (1915) pointed out that with the racist, financially motivated transatlantic slave trade, the world began "to invest in color prejudice and the color line began to pay dividends" (p. 708). Du Bois (1915) gave voice to words often heard and felt by Black and Brown people as Whites continued to enter spaces and places where Blacks resided, to tell Blacks what they are doing is wrong, and/or to take control of the spaces and places where Blacks resided.

> A white man is privileged to go to any land where advantage beckons and behave as he pleases . . . the white man is ruling black Africa for the white man's gain, and just as far as possible he is doing the same to colored races elsewhere.
>
> (Du Bois (1915, p. 77)

Democratic ruling grounded in moral dignity and respect for humanity, which should be the nature of governance in all spaces in America, was and is usurped by the social, political, and economic goals and practices of neoliberal policies and structural racism. This "soft despotism" (Tocqueville, 2004), while not as obvious as hard despotism and much like "the ruling of a schoolmaster than a tyrant" is counterproductive to the human potential of Black students and works to weaken their striving.

Teaching for Humanity at the Color Line

> High in the tower, where I sit above the loud complaining of the human sea, I know many souls that toss and whirl and pass, but none there are that intrigue me more than the Souls of White Folks.
>
> (Du Bois, 1920, p. 17)

In 1968, just a few weeks before his assassination, civil rights leader Martin Luther King Jr. referred to Du Bois's educational contribution in a speech honoring W. E. B. Du Bois: "Dr. Du Bois was not only an intellectual giant exploring the frontiers of knowledge, he was in the first place a teacher. He would have wanted his life to teach us something about our tasks of emancipation" (p. 77). Du Bois, per Martin Luther King Jr. (as well as many others), was an extraordinary teacher of America and the global community about democracy and the role of democratic deliberations and race in both keeping in place and reforming the unjust sovereignty of Whites in the United States and throughout Western Europe. Du Bois was an investigator of truth about race and class injustice. He did not hesitate to speak truth to power and to pursue racism despite the consequences. Du Bois stated in *The Philadelphia Negro* (1899),

> We must study, we must investigate, we must attempt to solve; and the utmost that the world can demand is, not lack of human interest and moral conviction, but rather the heart-quality of fairness, and an earnest desire for the truth despite its possible unpleasantness.
>
> (p. 3)

An extension of Du Bois's capacity as a great teacher was that he modeled new and different concepts, methods, and procedures to illuminate and explain the relationships between Blacks and Whites and other people of color. Du Bois was a mentor and teacher to Blacks and other people of color through his work and activism and a teacher to Whites about how they could contribute to the American democratic project by eliminating structural racism. Du Bois wanted Americans to understand that *racial equality did not represent the limit of American democracy*, but its beginning. Du Bois's teaching tools, as David Lewis (1993) posits, were many and varied—e.g., books, articles, speeches, journals, and a monthly magazine for children entitled *The Brownies' Books*. Du Bois saw his personhood—his agency, advocacy, and intelligence—as his most effective teaching tool.

Du Bois argued, "Children learn more from what you are than what you teach" (quoted in Dallas, 2012, p. 1). Du Bois's teaching strategies were also many and varied, the more significant were his passion, dedication, and his ability to explain his ideas in different ways—through letter writing, protest, history, art, music, contextual analysis, constant reflection, and engaging academically and socially with people from all walks of life. Du Bois's technique of mentoring included listening, caring, and speaking honestly. On the other hand, Du Bois was partial to the scholarship of men and ignored or would selectively include the scholarship of women, sometimes without crediting or citing them.

Much of Du Bois's method of teaching and technique of mentoring has influenced my teaching and mentoring of undergraduate and graduate students. Much like Du Bois, I discovered that social justice doesn't represent the limits of American democracy, but is the cornerstone of its well-being and prosperity. My purpose is to help undergraduates preparing to teach to look into themselves, to get to know the correct history of the United States, deal with their deficit thinking about students of color, encourage their "better angels," and understand that they can't teach what they don't know. Another purpose of mine is to help undergraduates to understand as Du Bois (1903/1994, 1920) contended, that the purpose of education was/is to be able to battle oppression, engage in self-improvement, and help bring about social change. Du Bois saw education as a weapon of resistance and a source of empowerment. It is because the undergraduate students I teach are preparing to be teachers, and the graduate students I teach are studying to become leaders in shaping US education policy and practice in a society that has failed to educate students of color and poor White students, that what I teach and what they take away is critical.

Over the years, with these thoughts in mind, when I prepare for the upcoming academic year, along with searching for new and better teaching materials and reassessing my teaching knowledge and strategies, I search for different sit-up-and-take-notice makers. Next, I discuss two publications I used during the past academic year and one publication I am considering using this upcoming academic year: *Souls of Black Folk* and "Souls of White Folk." Both were written by Du Bois, and I used them with my Social Justice and Multicultural Education Leadership class of 23 White and two Black school administrators who were studying to earn their doctorates.

Souls of Black Folk told the class about the educational striving, aspiration for political power, and demand for civil and human rights of Blacks since the 1600s. *Souls of Black Folk* said to the White administrators of schools where Black children attend that the Black bodies they saw before them are self-determined individuals who seek school knowledge so they can become spiritually and physically free. They understand they have freedom, but they don't have liberty. Additionally, the implicit messaging in *Souls* shifts. First, school leaders followed Du Bois's discussion of Blacks as a *problem* and an *outcast in their own house*. Next, they saw Blacks knowing and understanding the *problem*, but arguing that the *problem* is not of their own making, nor was enslavement, Jim Crow, or systematic racism. Du Bois then follows with a discussion of Whites' refusal to acknowledge race as a social construction. He argues that segregation and microaggressions are pervasive in social and political structures in the United States. *Souls of Black Folk* then raises the following question: "Why do Whites refuse to acknowledge the important roles Blacks played in the economic development of America as the premier global power?" In addition, Du Bois discusses Blacks' cultural gifts and contributions to the nation. Finally, *Souls of Black Folk* points out that Blacks are becoming independent, self-directed people. *Souls of Black Folk* says to administrators, it is your responsibility to see Black children, not as a *problem* or an "*outcast* and a stranger in mine own *house*," (Du Bois, 1903/1994, p. 3), but as young citizens eager for opportunities to learn and pursue their professional and social dreams. They want your help, just as you help White students, to become self-directed individuals, who develop the knowledge and skills to become socially, politically, and economically independent. They want to contribute to the American democratic project.

The school leaders took from "Souls of White Folk" a critique of racism that explains Whiteness as a social construction, racial identity, and White supremacy as a consolidation of White ethnicity. Du Bois's critique of racism, colonialism, and imperialism in "The Souls of White Folk," informed school leaders that Whiteness is not absolute, or "a sovereign, ahistorical, neutral subject that has absolute control" (Temple University, p. 6.) over social conditions and forces that give direction that dictate ways of knowing and doing. Du Bois explained that Whiteness is a problem and to reinscribe White entitlements is a direct contradiction to democratic fair play. bell hooks (1995), drawing upon Du Bois's theorizing of race and racism argues, "Those white people who want to continue the dominant-subordinate relationship so endemic to racist exploitation by insisting that we 'serve' them—that we do the work of challenging and changing their consciousness—are acting in bad faith" (pp. 193–194).

I also found "The Souls of White Folk" useful during the academic year of 2016 during the presidential campaign and days afterward for teaching my undergraduate class of 24 future teachers (22 White and 2 Mixed Race) during which racism, sexism, and White nationalism could be seen each day and night on television and read about in the printed media. Although "Souls of White Folk" was written after WWI and the Versailles Treaty of 1919, its message is meaningful for Americans, who continue to believe, as some Whites believed during the days of Jim Crow, that Blacks are less than White people, Blacks do not have an equal right to America's harvest of fruit and dreams, and that Whites can and should be the only leaders of America.

I see overt and covert racism many times each day and night whenever I take a break from this writing, where I am dealing with race and the ideologies and methodologies of racism. I also see and hear about racism on my university campus, particularly in the form of microaggressions and within forms of the color line that take place in Wisconsin public schools. Du Bois (1920) ties the development and establishment of racism to the economic development of America as a premier power and argued that "the eternal world-wide mark of meanness is color" (p. 42). "Souls of White Folk" gives my students a history lesson that they say they have not had. Some say they had difficulty reading "Souls of White Folk." Its history lesson and message makes them feel very uncomfortable. They wonder what will happen if they share the article with their friends or send a copy home to Dad and Mom. The essay points out that race became a tool for dehumanizing Blacks to make it not only easier but also okay to ignore the misery and suffering of Black people. Du Bois (1920) posits,

> This theory of human culture and its aims has worked itself through warp and woof of our daily thought with a thoroughness that few realize. Everything great, good, efficient, fair, and honorable is "white": everything mean, bad, blundering, cheating, and dishonorable is "yellow": a bad taste is "brown," and the devil is "black." The changes of this theme are continually rung in picture and story, in newspaper headings and moving-pictures, in sermon and school book, until, of course, the King can do no wrong—a White man is always right and a Black man has no rights which a white man is bound to respect.

> (p. 5)

Du Bois tells White folks that by participating in this false belief, they are dehumanizing themselves. I ask my teacher candidates—some, if not many, of whom will be future teachers in schools in urban spaces—how they felt about their White privilege. Some responded as Peggy McIntosh (1989) wrote; they have been learning about White privilege over their last two years on campus, but they have not come to fully deal with one of its corollary aspects: that White privilege and racism puts people of color at a disadvantage and puts Whites at an advantage. I asked the class, "What is your takeaway, now, after reading and discussing, 'Souls of White Folk?'" And, more importantly "What is in *your* 'soul?'" I asked them to confer with their elbow partners about Du Bois's essay and my questions, and write their responses on the board.

The activity generated many different types of responses. A few students welcomed Du Bois's essay, seeing it as illuminating, but about a half were especially cautious in what they wrote on the chalkboard and what they said to their Black professor, and still others tried to hide in silence. Du Bois (1920) acknowledged such stances from Whites when he wrote,

> Instead of standing as a great example of the success of democracy and the possibility of human brotherhood (and sisterhood) America has taken her place as an awful example of its pitfalls and failures, so far as black and brown and yellow people are concerned.
>
> (p. 28)

Finally, in *Souls of Black Folk* there is an essay titled "Of the Meaning of Progress" that shows the importance of education along with Du Bois's realization that education alone cannot overcome the racist attitude and beliefs that Whites have about Blacks. The essay speaks of the correlation between money and happiness. "Of the Meaning of Progress" is an autobiographical tale of irony. Du Bois begins the tale by stating, "Once upon a time I taught in the hills of Tennessee" (1903/1994, p. 37). The ten-page tale recounts Du Bois's return visit, more than a decade later, to the community and school in Wilson County, Tennessee, where he taught and lived during the summer break for two consecutive summers while a student at Fisk University. The United States is in an economic upswing brought on by more industries and businesses. The tale examines the *progress* of emancipated Blacks in Wilson by measuring their accomplishments since the time Du Bois left.

Josie, the central character, is a selfless aspiring person who is "willing to give all of life to make life broader, deeper, and fuller for her and hers" (Du Bois, 1903/1994, p. 38). Josie arguably symbolizes Black American humanity and Blacks' struggle and desire to go college in order to help themselves, their family members, and their communities. Josie met Du Bois when he came to Wilson County looking for a school. Josie tells Du Bois about a school in need of a teacher. The school has been without a teacher since the Civil War, two and a half decades earlier. Thus Black children had received little or no formal education, and their hopes and dreams of a better life after enslavement were being strangled. Josie befriended Du Bois, and her family becomes his family away from home for the two summers.

Wilson County was far different from Great Barrington where Du Bois grew up and attended school. In Wilson County, overt White supremacy and segregation were the normal way of life. Whites bluntly exercised their power and privilege, and in doing so, cut off opportunities for Blacks. Du Bois (1903/1994) posits, "Fell the awful shadow of the Veil" (p. 39). Du Bois's orientation to his teaching site was a reminder to him of his black skin and that his classical education and superior intelligence couldn't save him from having to remain in the Veil. At the orientation with the White commissioner of the local schools, Du Bois was made to feel the pangs of self-rejection; his "two-ness" and "double consciousness" confronted him. The commissioner, after hiring Du Bois to teach at the school Josie had told him about, invited him to dinner at his home. Once at the commissioner's home, Du Bois was informed that he would eat, after the commissioner's family had dined, in their kitchen, alone. This harsh, blunt reality, reminded Du Bois that he must live within the Veil and there was no acceptance of him in the White world, his elite college education notwithstanding.

Du Bois's schoolhouse was a broken-down log hut where corn was previously stored. There were no doors or windows. Furniture was scarce; there was a blackboard and three boards nailed together served as Du Bois's desk. Du Bois borrowed a chair each morning from the women who owned the land and returned it each night. The students' seats were rough plank benches without backs, and at times without legs. Thirty-one miles from Fisk University, Du Bois was witness to the meanness and normalization of the color line for Black children.

When Du Bois saw his students for the first time on a hot July summer day coming down the dusty road to the schoolhouse with Josie leading the way, he looked at their solemn faces and bright eyes and began to tremble. Some of his trembling may have come because this was his first time teaching, but I believed it came because Du Bois knew the students came with hope and dreams. They symbolized the way Du Bois hoped Black youth everywhere would approach education, and they would see it as the development of power and ideal. As his students entered the log schoolhouse and took their seats, Du Bois (1903/1994) observed, "There they sat, nearly thirty of them, on the rough benches . . . the little feet bare and swinging, the eyes full of expectation . . . and the hands grasping Webster's blue-back spelling-book . . ." (p. 40). They had come to get an education, to take advantage of the opportunity that their grandparents had died for and their parents were advocating take place.

In "Of the Meaning of Progress," Du Bois writes of his love of his school, the joy he discovered in teaching, and the "fine faith the children had in wisdom" (p. 40). He tells of how he and his students read and spelled together, wrote, picked flowers, and sang. They were happily engaged in learning, and learning was fun. He also tells of their wide eyes as they listened to stories of the world beyond the hills where America was making its power and influence felt around the world. The "progressive era" of industrialization was increasingly developing in the United States, but the *progress*, including the educational progress of his students, Du Bois would discover would come slowly, and the progress that came would come with a great deal of difficulty inspired by racism. Du Bois describes times when the number of students in his class would dwindle. Boys were absent because they were needed to pick crops. Money and livelihood was put first before education, and working mostly as sharecroppers kept Blacks from ever having enough money to pursue their educational dreams.

On the weekends, Du Bois would stay with different students' families. His favorite place to stay was with Josie's family. There he would sit on the porch eating peaches. He would listen to Josie's mother tell of how Josie had bought a sewing machine and how she worked in the winter for four dollars a month. Josie's mother told Du Bois of how Josie longed to go away to school, but the family could never save enough money to allow her to go. The other families, Du Bois learned, also didn't have money to send their children to college, and in Wilson County, money-making opportunities for Blacks were meager.

For two summers, Du Bois lived in rural agricultural Wilson County. He observed the girls looking at the hill "in wistful longing" for a better life and realizing their path to achieve a better life was narrow and filled with barriers. The boys weren't any better, but at times they would take off for Alexandria—"a straggling, lazy village of houses, churches, and shops," (Du Bois, 1903/1994, p. 41). Writing about the community, Du Bois (1903/1994) describes hardship and Black people's partial awareness of opportunities beyond where they lived, because of the veil and racism.

> I have called my tiny community a world, and so its isolation made it; and yet there was among us, but a half-awakened common consciousness, sprung from common joy and grief, at burial, birth, or wedding; from a common hardship in poverty, poor land, and low wages; and, above all, from the sight of the Veil that hung between us and Opportunity.
>
> (p. 41)

When Du Bois returned to Wilson Country, after his ten years' absence, to see how his students and their families were making out, he discovered that Josie had died from overwork. She had been cheated, by the absence of democracy in Wilson County, of the opportunity to get an education. Josie's mother explained to Du Bois that working hard each day for very low wages in order to provide for the family and walking nine miles to visit her brother in jail wore her down. Du Bois's students' families, on a whole, were not doing well; several girls had young children and no future for themselves or for their children. The boys, now young Black men, were trapped in the cycle of limited opportunity. Sharecropping doomed them to debt and a short life. Du Bois sadly discovered the passion his students once had for education had been destroyed. To live in a society that denied opportunity and paid only minimal wages meant Blacks could not focus on education. Jacobs (2014) observes today, "Those U.S. counties that in the past exhibited a higher slave share over population turn out to be still more unequal in the present day" (p. 1). Du Bois (1903) posits, "How hard a thing is life to the lowly, and yet how human and real!" (p. 45). Ben was a case in point:

> There was Sam Carlon, an impudent old skinflint, who had definite notions about "niggers," and hired Ben for a summer and would not pay him. Then the hungry boy gathered his sacks together, and in broad daylight went into Carlon's corn; and when the hard-fisted farmer set upon him, the angry boy flew at him like a beast. Doc Burke saved a murder and a lynching that day.
>
> (p. 44)

The new schoolhouse for students, in comparison to Du Bois's old school, was only slightly better. The poor construction and resources put into the new school reflected the county's negative attitude about the education of Blacks and their future. Du Bois writes, "The log school house was gone. In its place stood Progress; and Progress, I understand, is necessarily ugly . . . . (p. 43). That "progress is necessarily ugly" is a statement that exemplifies progress for Blacks in Wilson County and progress for Blacks in America. "One step forward, two steps back."

"Of the Meaning of Progress" is a story in which many who work in urban areas may discover a close connection, although the history and geography are different. Josie embodied striving and resiliency and the struggles of Blacks against racism to achieve a better life. Josie's struggle is indicative of the rugged challenges many Blacks encountered wherever and whenever they lived. Du Bois's students and their family members represented many Blacks in urban areas writ large. There are only a few accomplishments and many difficulties as racism, neoliberal politics, and a lack of community support were given to the individual. Happiness and joy are hard to locate. The schoolhouse, before and after, in "Of the Meaning of Progress" is much like the schools in many urban areas today; they need modernization, full resource allocation, and teachers who are well educated in C&I, and who understand the students they are teaching.

Progress, for Blacks, which is more than change, was not what Whites in Wilson County wanted to take place for Black children whose parents had endured enslavement and had made America a leader on the world's economic stage. Whereas change is not *progress*, progress does require change. For Blacks in the eighteenth and nineteenth centuries, *progress* included triumphing over the ignorance of social Darwinist and eugenicist theorizing of the inferiority of Blacks and the elimination of White fear, terror, segregation, and Jim Crow. *Progress* also required the development of total quality of life for Blacks that included being a part of America's rising industrialization, having school for an entire academic year and not just a few weeks, opportunities for good jobs, access to quality health treatment and the ballot, and total respect for Black humanity.

Conclusion

The story line and characters from "Of the Meaning of Progress" were only a part of the many ways Du Bois discussed the *progress* of Blacks in the face of strong White resistance. Du Bois's strategies for discussing and promoting *progress* for Blacks included other essays, such as "Of the Coming of John," sociological data (e.g., *The Philadelphia Negro;* "Of the Wings of Atlanta" and "Of the Training of Black Men"), preparation and hope for the future; (*the Atlanta Universities of the Negro,* see the *Journal of Negro Education, 1957; and, running for public office*).

To conclude the tale "Of the Meaning of Progress," Du Bois states, "My journey was done, and behind me lay hill and dale, and Life and Death. How shall man measure Progress there where the dark-faced Josie lies? How many heartfuls of sorrow shall balance a bushel of wheat?" (p. 64), as he speaks of his students' desperate need to secure money for food and shelter in place of pursuing an education. And then Du Bois lets the readers know that, at that time in the late 1800s, and perhaps for longer, *progress* for Blacks is not social change; their only change, or the predominate change they see in their lives, is brought about by death, marriages, and babies.

Progress for Blacks necessitates social equality, the ballot, respect for the humanity of Blacks, and full recognition and acceptance that Blacks have many gifts to give to society. Thus Du Bois with glee, but sadly knowing about the journey before him, which he faces with optimism, writes: "Thus sadly musing, *I rode to Nashville in the Jim Crow car*" (p. 64, my emphasis).

When I visit communities and schools in urban spaces and consider *progress*, I, somewhat like Du Bois, know and understand that *progress* in urban areas for decades upon decades has been a fairy tale.

Final Thoughts

The Sunshine of Du Bois Needs to Continue to Shine

Throughout the writing of *Du Bois and Education*, each morning when I awoke to begin my day of research and writing, I thought of it as having a study session with Willie. Du Bois's study of ideologies (e.g., White superiority, Black inferiority, White privilege) and methodologies (segregation, microaggressions, voter suppression) of racism and their effects became clearer each day. Du Bois's analysis that race was socially constructed and the differences between races—superiority and inferiority—was based on flawed science that Whites used to keep Blacks as three-fifths individuals in the eyes of America and the world was significant to the study of race and racism. Also, Du Bois's analysis of the ideology of social class—that is, membership in upper-class constitutes receiving opportunities and privileges and blaming people who are in a lower social class for their own circumstances—is significant in this time when society is divided into the haves and have-nots. Additionally, Du Bois's analysis of the ideologies of education—"an educated citizenry is a vital requisite for our survival as a free people" (Jefferson, n. d. in Berkes, 2010, p. 1), schooling is the gateway to the American dream, schooling of Blacks should not challenge White supremacy or lead to economic competition with Whites (Washington, 1895), and education is the pathway to full citizenship and true freedom (Du Bois, 1903/1994) is necessary to those studying urban schools.

Du Bois's multiple methods of resisting and challenging racism—scholarly magazines, newspaper articles, books, research reports, speeches, talks, forming organizations, engaging with people, and so forth—are excellent for social justice and multicultural advocates. Du Bois's approaches to first understanding and deconstructing the racist ideologies that guided Whites' resistance to Blacks, along with his approaches to understanding and deconstructing racist methodologies, would be valuable to those studying race and racism in historical and geographic contexts today.

I started the journey toward writing *Du Bois and Education* years ago as a child listening to stories about race and racism. I continue to believe that many, if not most, of Du

Bois's approaches to the study of race and racism, along with his beliefs and ideas, are needed today. This became especially evident as I experienced and observed current conditions and events, such as a divided country's reactions to the 2016 US presidential election, the continuous social assault on minoritized people, and the spread of hatred and mutual distrust across the globe. In addition, the normalization of neoliberal ideologies and practices, and the reassertion of White patriarchy and Whiteness assured me that Du Bois's ideas are needed in the here and now. Tabb (2003) argues,

> Dr. Du Bois understood the impacts of what today, we call neoliberalism, its damages, its causes, the interests it serves, and the way it divides the working class and undercuts the progressive movements with horrible consequences at home and abroad.
>
> (p. 1)

The fight to increase the number of people who believe in the full humanity of all people will be a serious challenge in this second and upcoming third decade of the twenty-first century. To push back and to discredit pervasive lies and distortions of the ideologies and methodologies of racism that serve Whites' self-interest demands drawing on Du Bois's catalog of work against racist ideology and behavior. Du Bois wrote and narrated illuminating accounts of race and racism and their harsh effects on American Blacks and Whites. Du Bois's analysis of race and racism during Reconstruction, industrialization, post-industrialization, World War I and II, the Holocaust, and Civil Rights Movements are analytic narratives second to none and will continue be useful in the challenges ahead.

Fighters for social justice are aware that social media has expanded the public square, and this allows manifestations of racial hatred to be streamlined to appeal to different localities. Communication between speakers and listeners, for example, are targeted with a crafted ideology of racism and strategies of delivery to influence specific constituencies about how, for example, one group, often minoritized groups, are taking opportunities away from Whites. It is argued that minoritized groups are making America too brown and snatching away those things that were once considered white and right. America, it is argued, is not what it used to be. Du Bois understood the chameleon-like "Souls of White Folk" who sprout the ideology of racism. He spoke out passionately against racial strategies used to make Blacks inferior and Whites superior in favor of humanity of all people. Du Bois crafted essays to respond to manufactured claims of White superiority and false interpretations of the intellectual abilities of Blacks sprouted by hate groups, including southern segregationists and liberals who didn't fully believe in racial equality, and political and government leaders such as segregationist President Woodrow Wilson.

Furthermore, with all that we are seeing in the world— fake news articles, dissemination of misinformation, people with cognitive distance about news that doesn't support their views, a large reduction in the number of investigative journalists uncovering stories, and a lack of historical knowledge— Du Bois's critique of ideologies and methodologies of race and racism could provide insights into how to confront and challenge these current efforts.

In addition, my study sessions with Willie taught me that Du Bois did not hesitate—put off or leave to someone else—to fiercely and boldly challenge racism. "The problem of the twentieth is the problem of the color line," Du Bois (1900) exclaimed to the entire world at a time when Blacks throughout the world were aggressively under attack by racist ideologies and methodologies. In his fight of resistance, I discovered, if organizational means to challenge racism were not at his disposal, he worked to develop organizations and communication sources and to make known to the public efforts of resistance. Just as Du Bois used the tools at his disposal (NAACP, speaking out) and his tireless efforts to shine a light on racism, today, I believe, Du Bois would be using every modern tool of technology to "out" racist behavior and actions for what they are and who they benefit. Du Bois, I believe, would have organized and been vocal about "Make America Great Again," which essentially translates into "make America white again." Du Bois would have challenged the press for not calling out racist statements during the 2016 election more boldly. Du Bois would label coded language and dog whistles for what they are and for whose interest is being served, as he did in "The Souls of White Folk."

The history of America, unfortunately, is one that when Blacks achieve progress (the Voting Rights Act; the election of President Obama), usually what follows is White backlash (voter suppression and birther movement). In sessions with Willie, you see how historical analysis of events are used to support arguments against racist ideologies and methodologies. In *Darkwater* (1920), for example, Du Bois challenges the ideologies and methodologies of democracy that accept some of its citizens as three-fifths, Europe's exploitation of Africa as America sat quietly by after World War I, and, although too few, his robust challenges against the oppression of Black women. Du Bois (1920) stated,

> I shall forgive the white south much in its final judgement day: I shall forgive its slavery, for slavery is a world-old habit; I shall forgive its

fighting for a well-lost cause, and for remembering that struggle with tender tears; I shall forgive its so-called 'pride of race,' the passion of its hot blood, and even its dear, old, laughable strutting and posing; but one thing I shall never forgive, neither in this world nor the world to come: its wanton and continued and persistent insulting of the black womanhood which it sought and seeks to prostitute to its lust.

(p. 1)

Although, Du Bois faced ideologies and methodologies of racism continually throughout his life, he remained optimistic that Blacks and other people of good conscious would stand up and push back. Du Bois's optimism is needed now as many fighters against racism are feeling the backlash from the 2016 presidential election and growing global unrest.

I conclude *Du Bois and Education* with a bit of Du Bois's optimism because among many young people—Black, White, and others—there is interest in "discussions with Willie." Whenever I'm asked the question, "Carl, what book are you writing now?" and I respond *Du Bois and Education*, the response is met with anticipation more so than any other book I have written. People today, especially young scholars and community activists, want to know more about William Edward Burghardt Du Bois, "Willie." They are eager to learn about the man and his work, and how his ideas and ways of doing would be helpful to them personally and their work. Evidence of Du Bois's optimism I took away from one of his final public statements, "The Negro and Young People" (Du Bois, 1961), when he observed youth taking initiative. Du Bois (1961) graciously remarked at the time that they didn't need his help. Also, although near the end of his life when he went to Ghana to live, his work against racism and his work to establish the worth and humanity of Blacks never paused. At the time of his death in Accra, Ghana, at the age of 95, Du Bois was working on the *Encyclopedia Africana*. The encyclopedia was a project Du Bois wanted to undertake for many years.

Du Bois never quit in his fight against the ideologies and methodologies of racism, and as I look back to my childhood and youth in Bronzeville and recall the storytelling I heard, and people I met, I never heard one say, "It is time for me to stop." *Du Bois and Education*, besides being an interactive learning experience, was an opportunity for me to more fully appreciate and embrace Du Bois's optimism. I echo Du Bois's (1920) optimism in the closing of *Du Bois and Education*: "What a world this will be when human possibilities are freed, when we discover each other, when the stranger is no longer the potential criminal and the certain inferior!" (p. 103).

References

Anderson, M. D. (February 16, 2016). The promise of integrated schools. *The Atlantic*. www.theatlantic.com/education/archive/2016/02/promise-of-integrated-schools/462681/ (accessed 3 March 2016).

Anthony, K. (2014). Neighborhood Effects: The Influence on School Closure and Openings. *Chicago Policy Review*. Available online: http://chicagopolicyreview.org/2014/04/28/neighborhood-effects-the-influence-on-school-closures-and-openings (accessed 24 May 2016).

Baldwin, J. (2017). Quoted in *I am not your Negro*. Film. Directed by Raoul Peck. Written by James Baldwin.

BlackDemographics.com. (2015). Black population: 46.3, 14.4% of USA. http://blackdemographics.com/. 3/15/17.

Byrd, W. M. and Clayton, L. A. (March 2001). Race, medicine, and health care in the United States: A historical survey. *Journal National Medical Association*, 93(3) (Suppl), 11s–34S. www.ncbi.nlm.nih.gov/pmc/articles/PMC2593958/ (accessed 12 January 2016).

Cannon, K. G. (1995). *Womanism and the souls of black community*. New York: Continuum.

CBS Chicago (2016). Racial Profiling. Available online: http://chicago.cbslocal.com/tag/racial-profiling (accessed 10 November 2016).

Center for Public Education (2012). The United States of Education: The Changing Demographics of the United States and Their Schools. Available online: www.centerforpubliceducation.org/You-May-Also-Be-Interested-In-landing-page-level/Organizing-a-School-YMABI/The-United-States-of-education-The-changing-demographics-of-the-United-States-and-their-schools.html (accessed 2 March 2017).

Dallas, C. (2012). *A legacy in poems: Bridging the gap.* United Kingdom: Xlibris Corp.

Du Bois, W. E. B. (1897). The conservation of races. The American Nedgro Academy Occasional Papers, No, 2. Washington, D. C. Published by the Academy. www.webdubois.org/dbConsrvOfRaces.html. 3/7/17.

Du Bois, W. E. B. (1899). *The Philadelphia Negro.* Philadelphia: University of Pennsylvania Press.

Du Bois, W. E. B. (1903/1994). *The souls of black folk.* New York: Dover.

Du Bois, W. E. B. (October, 1904). Credo. In Irene Diggs, "Du Bois and Children." www.jstor.org/stable/274501?seq=1#page_scan_tab_contents.3/19/17.

Du Bois, W. E. B. (1915). *The Negro.* Philadelphia: University of Pennsylvania Press.

Du Bois, W. E. B. (May 1915). The African Roots of War. *The Atlantic Monthly* 115(5), 707–714. Available online: www.google.com/#q=Du+Bois,+W.+E.+B.+(May+1915).+%E2%80%9CThe+African+roots+of+war.%E2%80%9D+The+Atlantic+Monthly+115,+5,+707-714 (accessed 7 May 2017).

Du Bois, W. E. B. (1919). The True Brownies. *The Crisis*, October, 285–286.

Du Bois, W. E. B. (1920). *Darkwater: Voices from within the veil.* Mineloa, NY: Dover.

Du Bois, W. E. B. (1924). *The gift of black folks.* Boston: Stratford.

Du Bois, W. E. B. (1926). Criteria of Negro Art. Available online: www.coreknowledge.org/mimik/mimik_uploads/documents/297/Du%20Bois%20WEB%20%20Criteria%20of%20Negro%20Art.pdf (accessed 14 November 2016).

Du Bois, W. E. B. (1934). A Negro Nation Within a Nation. *Current History*, 42, 268.

Du Bois, W. E. B. (1930). Editorial. *The Crisis.* 353. Quoted in Carol M Taylor (June 1981). W. E. B. Du Bois's Challenge to Scientific Racism. *Journal of Black Studies*, 11(4), 449–460.

Du Bois, W. E. B. (1935). Does the Negro Need Separate Schools? *Journal of Negro Education*, 4(3), 328–335.

Du Bois, W. E. B. (1940a). *Dusk of dawn: An essay toward an autobiography*. New York: Oxford.

Du Bois, W. E. B. (1940b). *The world of W. E. B. Du Bois: A quotation sourcebook*. Santa Barbara, CA: Greenwood Publishing Group.

Du Bois, W. E. B. (1961). The Negro and Young People. *W. E. B. DuBois: A Recorded Autobiography, Interview with Moses Asch*. Available online: www.amazon.com/The-Negro-and-Young-People/dp/B000S3CI7M (accessed 8 December 2016).

Du Bois, W. E. B. (2001). *The Negro*. Mineola, NY: Dover Publications.

Encyclopedia of Chicago (n.d.). Chicago Housing Authority. Available online: www.encyclopedia.chicagohistory.org/pages/253.html (accessed 14 August 2016).

Homel, M. W. (1984). *Down from equality: Black children and the public school, 1920–1941*. Chicago: University of Illinois Press.

hooks, b. (1995). *Killing rage: Ending racism*. New York: H. Holt and Co.

Jacobs, T. (2014). Slavery's Legacy: Race-Based Economic Inequality. *Pacific Standard*. Available online: https://psmag.com/economics/slaverys-legacy-race-based-economic-inequality-83854 (accessed 10 March 2016).

Jefferson, T. (n. d.) See Anna Berkes (2010). Thomas Jefferson Encyclopedia. An educated citizenry is a vital requisite for our survival as a free people (spurious quotation). www.monticello.org/site/jefferson/educated-citizenry-vital-requisite-our-survival-free-people-spurious-quotation. Accessed 4/4/17.

Johnson, R. C. (2014). Long-Run Impacts of School Desegregation & School Quality on Adult Attainments. National Bureau of Economic Research. Available online: http://tinyurl.com/katral3 (accessed 15 August 2016).

Khan, M. (June 7, 2016). Black students nearly 4x as likely to be suspended. *USA Today*. http://abcnews.go.com/US/black-students-times-.suspended/story?id=39670502 (accessed 10 June 2016).

King, M. L. Jr. (1968). Honoring D. Du Bois. no 2, 1968. In E. Cooper & Constance Pohl Freedom Reader (Eds.), *Prophets in their own country*. Boulder, CO: Westview Press.

Kirp, D. L. (2012). Making Schools Work. *The New York Times*, May 19, Available online: http://tinyurl.com/osmyh77 (accessed 5 August 2016).

Knupfer, A. M. (2006). *The Chicago Black Renaissance and Women's Activism*. Urbana, IL: University of Illinois Press.

Kozol, J. (1967). *Death at an early age*. Boston: Houghton Mifflin.

Kozol, J. (1991). *Savage inequalities: Children in America's schools*. New York: Crown Publishing.

Lewis, D. L. (2001). *W. E. B. Du Bois: The fight for equality and the American century, 1919–1963*. New York: Henry Holt.

McAuliffe, D. (2013). Did Integration Hurt Black America? Available online: www.theliberatedmind.com/2013/06/did-integration-hurt-black-america. html (accessed 5 August 2016).

McIntosh, P. (1989). *White privilege: Unpacking the invisible knapsack*. S.l.

Means, A. (2008). Neoliberalism and the Politics of Disposability: Education, Urbanization, and Displacement in the New Chicago. *Journal of Critical Education Policy Studies*, 6(1), 1–22. Available online: www. jceps.com/wp-content/uploads/PDFs/06-1-03.pdf (accessed 19 May 2016).

Mishra, P. (2016). The Globalization of Rage. *Foreign Affairs*. Available online: www.foreignaffairs.com/articles/world/2016-10-17/globalization (accessed 17 December 2016).

Morrison, T. (1998, March). From an Interview on Charlie Rose. Public Broadcasting Service. Retrieved from www.youtube.com/watch?v=F4vlGvKpT1c (accessed 7 May 2017).

Olson, J. (2005). WEB Du Bois and the Race Concept. Taylor and Francis Online. Available online: www.tandfonline.com/doi/abs/10.1080/10999940500265532?journalCode=usou20 (accessed 2 February 2016).

Peterson, B. (1998). History and Race. *The Baltimore Sun*, January 8. Available online: http://articles.baltimoresun.com/1998-01-08/news/1998008092_1_racism-lovejoy-history-textbook (accessed 5 November 2016).

Pinderhughes, D. M. (1987). *Race and ethnicity in Chicago Politics: A reexamination of pluralist theory*. Urbana: University of Illinois Press.

Pirofski, K. I. (2015). Race, gender, and disability in today's children literature. Critical Multicultural Pavilion. www.edchange.org/multicultural/papers/literature2.html.3/19/17.

Reilly, K. (2016). Majority of Chicago Police Shooting Victims are Black Men or Boys: Report. Available online: http://time.com/4469377/chicago-police-shootings-black-men (accessed 26 November 2016).

Semuels, A. (June 19, 2015). Has America given up on the dream of racial integration? *The Atlantic*. www.theatlantic.com/business/archive/2015/06/segregation-2015/396167/ (accessed 23 June 2016).

Sustar, L. (2013). Behind the Racist School Closings Agenda. socialistworker. org. March 26. Available online: http://socialistworker.org/2013/03/26/behind-the-racist-school-closings-agenda.

Tabb, W. K. (2003). Du Bois vs. Neoliberalism. *Monthly Review*, 55, 6 November. Available online: http://monthlyreview.org/2003/11/01/du-bois-vs-neoliberali.

Taylor, C. M. (1981). W. E. B. Du Bois's challenge to scientific racism. *Journal of Black Studies*. 11, 4 (June). pp. 449–460.

Taylor, K.-Y. (2012). Challenging Jim Crow Schools in Chicago. Socialist-worker.org. Available online: https://socialistworker.org/2012/02/22/jim-crow-schools-in-chicago (accessed 20 May 2016).

Teaching for Change (2015). *Finding multicultural children's books.* Available online: www.teachingforchange.org/books/multicultural-childrens-books (accessed 2 March 2017).

Temple University (n.d.). Flipping the Script. Available online: www.temple.edu/tempress/chapters_1800/2203_ch1.pdf (accessed 22 August 2016).

The 1930s: Education: Overview. In J. S. Baughman, et al. (Eds.), *American decades* (Vol. 4, pp. 1930–1939). Detroit: Gale, 2001. *U.S. History in Context.* Web. 2 August 2016. Available online: http://ic.galegroup.com/ic/uhic/ReferenceDetailsPage/ReferenceDetailsWindow?query.

Tocqueville, A. de (2004). *Democracy in America.* New York: Penguin Putman.

Toppo, G. (June 7, 2016). Black students nearly 4x as likely to be suspended. USA TODAY. www.usatoday.com/story/news/2016/06/07/black-students-nearly-4x-likely-suspended/85526458/. Accessed 3/28/17.

US Department of Education, National Center for Education Statistics 2010–2011. (2016). Closed Schools. Available online: https://nces.ed.gov/fastfacts/display.asp?id=619 (accessed March 2016).

Ven den Berghe, W. (1967). *Race and racism: A comparative perspective.* New York: Wiley.

Washington, B. T. (1895). Cast down your bucket where you are. In T. Booker (Ed.), *Washington's Atlanta compromise speech.* http://historymatters.gmu.edu/d/88 (accessed 20 November 2016).

Williams, E. (1944). *Capitalism and slavery.* Chapel Hill, NC: University of North Carolina Press.

Wolters, R. (2014). *The long crusade, 1967–2014.* Whitefish, MT: Washington Summit Publishers.

Wright, R. (1941). *12 million voices.* New York: Thunder's Mouth Press.

INDEX